Aesop in England
*The Transmission of Motifs in
Seventeenth-Century Illustrations of*
Aesop's Fables

Aesop in England

The Transmission of Motifs in Seventeenth-Century Illustrations of Aesop's Fables

Edward Hodnett

Published for the Bibliographical Society
of the University of Virginia

by the University Press of Virginia
Charlottesville

THE UNIVERSITY PRESS OF VIRGINIA
Copyright © 1979 by the Rector and Visitors
of the University of Virginia

First published 1979

Library of Congress Cataloging in Publication Data
Hodnett, Edward, 1901–
  Aesop in England.
  Bibliography: p. 67.
  Includes index.
    1. Illustration of books—17th century—England—
Bibliography. 2. Illustration of books—Themes, motifs
—Bibliography. 3. Aesopus. Fabulae—Illustrations—
Bibliography. I. Virginia. University. Bibliographi-
cal Society. II. Title.
Z1023.H68 [NC978]   741.64′0942   78-15268
ISBN 0-8139-0772-1

Printed in the United States of America

To the Memory of Paul Murray Kendall
Teacher, Scholar, Friend

Contents

Figures

Preface

This study was undertaken because there was no other way to find the answers to questions arising in the course of writing a book about Francis Barlow, the first major English book illustrator. Besides accomplishing its specific aim, it may be of use for reference by biliographers, literary scholars, art historians, and librarians, as well as by persons directly concerned with book illustration. It may also be of practical use to scholars pursuing problems in any one of those innumerable literary and artistic works in which Aesopic fable material appears. Finally, this investigation of the graphic aspects of Aesopic fables may encourage more scholarly study both of the fable in England and of the relationship between image and text in English literature.

In addition to those persons whose help is acknowledged at appropriate places in the text, I must thank David Du Vivier of Princeton, New Jersey; Professor Joseph Katz of the University of South Carolina; George D. Painter, formerly of the British Library; Professor Hans-Joachim Zimmermann of the University of Heidelberg; and John F. Andrews of the Folger Shakespeare Library for reading the manuscript and making valuable suggestions. David L. Paisey and the young men and women of his North Library staff in the British Library were, as always, as friendly as they were courteous and helpful.

I gratefully acknowledge the use of photographic material from the following sources:

Figures. British Library (by permission of the British Library Board): 1, 5, 7, 15, 16; Folger Shakespeare Library (by permission of the Director): 2, 9; Library of Congress: 3, 4, 6, 8, 10–14, 17–20.

Plates. British Library (by permission of the British Library Board): 1-6, 8-14, 16-23, 25-32, 34-43, 45-50; Bodleian Library (by permission of the Curators): 7, 15, 24, 33, 44.

                                                    E.H.

Chevy Chase, Maryland

Introduction

1. Aesop in England

Aesop is England's most universal literary figure. He is as alive today as he was in Caxton's day. For nearly five hundred years English printed versions called *Aesop's Fables* have been read by little children, ordinary folk, and learned scholars. "Hawks and doves," "dog in the manger," "sour grapes," "lion's share," "shoulder to the wheel," "blowing hot and cold," "crying wolf"—scores of allusions to the fables live in our everyday speech and newspaper headlines as they have lived so vigorously in English literature. Few English literary works have appeared in as many editions as *Aesop,* and from Caxton's first edition in 1484 to the most recent they have been illustrated in nearly every medium and by all sorts of artists, including some of the finest illustrators who have ever worked in England. Among them, the seventeenth-century etchers Wenceslaus Hollar and Francis Barlow are the most distinguished.

The complex story of Aesop and the several collections of fables that have clustered about his name is readily available and cannot be retold here. Before 1700 in England the customary title *Fables of Aesop* or *Aesop's Fables* applies consistently enough to the body of fables (without the Italian tales) translated by Dr. Heinrich Steinhöwel for Johann Zainer's Ulm edition of ca. 1476. It is therefore used here in this generic sense, not as the title of a single literary work.

William Caxton and His Followers

England could hardly have found a better man than William Caxton to be its first printer, or more exactly printer, translator, editor, and publisher. He was English (his chief associates and immediate followers were all aliens), and he knew and loved English literature and included Chaucer and Malory among the authors whose works he chose to publish. Along with standard religious works and books of knowledge, his list contained belles lettres such as the *Aeneid, Four Sons of Aymon, Paris and Vienne, Reynard the Fox*—and *Fables of Esope*. Yet he had one weakness: he never showed anything like the same independence of judgment and discriminating taste in his illustrations, although he had lived for years in Bruges, the home not only of great painting but also of beautiful illuminated manuscripts to which he had access. True, in London when he returned to set up his printing press beside the door of the Chapter House of Westminster Abbey, war had diverted money and talent and interest away from art. He printed a number of books before he allowed some inexperienced hand to hack out eleven miserable woodcuts for the *Myrroure of the Worlde* (1481). He proceeded to load his books for several years thereafter with woodcut illustrations, but the few good ones he owned were second-hand blocks from the Continent.

Caxton depended largely on one man to copy continental illustrations for him, probably one of the printers, possibly a local craftsman such as a goldsmith or a woodworker. This "hand" was a fair cutter but no expert, a simple mechanic who never pretended to be original or ever thought of himself as an illustrator. He and an even less skilled associate cut an impressive 186 broad blocks for Caxton's folio *Fables of Esope* (Westminster, 26 March 1484). His Hawk, Doves, & Kite (fig. 1) is typical. Caxton translated his version from Julien Macho's first French translation of the Steinhöwel collection printed by Nicholas Philippe and Marcus Reinhard (Lyons, 1480), and he based his woodcuts on the Lyons facsimile copies of Zainer's blocks as they appeared again in Anton Sorg's Augsburg edition (1480?). The only extant example of this first French edition is in Tours, but Claude Dalbanne has reproduced the same woodcuts as they appear in the third

1. Anonymous. *Fables of Esope*. William Caxton, tr. London: William Caxton, 1484.

edition, with a few incidental changes, printed by Matthew Husz (Lyons, 1486). The German, French, and English blocks vary slightly, and they include about three dozen designs not used in the later English editions that we deal with here. The changes by Caxton's hands are trivial—the prim substitution of a skull for a naked female torso to illustrate the fable of the wolf and the idol is the only conspicuous one. Furthermore, Caxton's illustrations follow the Lyons facsimiles in the same order. Partly for that reason, they are not recorded in the Concordance later in this study. They would take up a good deal of space and would be invariably followed by a symbol indicating Zainer as their certain source. The main reason for not including them in the Concordance, however, is that they are not part of the line of descent to the seventeenth-century English *Aesop*s.

Wynkyn de Worde, who was Caxton's assistant and

succeeded to his business, was the most enthusiastic early printer of illustrated books in England. Yet no *Aesop's Fables* is credited to him, only an unillustrated grammar based on the fables. This is odd, because he must have taken over the 186 *Aesop* blocks along with the rest of Caxton's stock. Even more odd, at the Huntington Library is a copy of an edition (1497) printed by his rival Richard Pynson and illustrated with Caxton's woodcuts. But then Pynson brought out another edition (1500?), for which he had a complete series of copies of Caxton's illustrations made. Smaller and squarer, they are somewhat better looking than Caxton's, but the motifs are wholly Zainer's. Since one of Caxton's blocks turns up later in a de Worde book, one may suspect that de Worde shared the (1497) edition with Pynson—that he contributed the blocks, and Pynson the printing. No example with de Worde's colophon survives, but this is not an unusual phenomenon of early printing. In 1507 de Worde supplied the cuts for the *Boke Named the Royall,* which he shared with Pynson, and in the same year both he and Pynson contributed cuts to a shared edition of the *Legenda aurea.*

Wherever I have indicated Zainer as the source for any later English *Aesop* illustrations, the immediate source might conceivably be Caxton or Pynson rather than a continental edition, but the probability seems slim.

No other sixteenth-century English edition of *Aesop* is of the slightest interest for its illustrations or likely to be the source for later illustrators.

Marcus Gheeraerts the Elder

The first known artist resident in England who can be called a practicing book illustrator is Marcus Gheeraerts the elder (ca. 1520–ca.1590?), often confused with his son of the same name, a leading Elizabethan portrait painter (1561/62–1635/36). Marcus the elder, fleeing from Bruges because of his Protestant beliefs, came to London in 1568. There can be no reasonable doubt that he was the etcher of the twenty illustrations in Jan van der Noot's *Théâtre,* printed by John Day in a Dutch edition in 1568 and in a French edition a month later. Gheeraerts worked in London for nine years; then following the Pacification of Ghent in 1577 he worked in Antwerp until 1586, when he returned to London. His only known signed works during his London years are a long nine-plate etched print, "Procession of the Order of the Garter" (1576), and two drawings. There is reason to think that he was the designer of the woodcut illustrations in two English books—Stephen Bateman's *A Christall Glasse* (John Day, 1569) and Raphael Holinshed's *Chronicles of England, Scotlande, and Irelande* (Henry Bynneman, 1577). (Shakespeare is said to have used the enlarged but unillustrated second edition.) As illustrator of Day's edition of the *Théâtre,* Marcus Gheeraerts the elder becomes the first known etcher to practice in England and the first identifiable illustrator of belles lettres printed in England. Apart from the matter of precedence, his etched illustrations are important because they introduced to the English a naturalism not known in their early woodcuts.

Gheeraerts's direct influence on English book illustration is even more important. In 1567, a few months before he fled Bruges, he brought out *De warachtighe fabulen der dieren,* a Flemish version of Aesop's fables by Edewaerd de Dene, a lawyer of Bruges. The 107 illustrations in it are among the earliest examples of extensive use of the medium of etching to illustrate a book. The lifelike birds and animals and the realistic human figures, costumes, and settings made Gheeraerts's plates popular throughout Europe. Gheeraerts added 18 new ones in *Esbatement moral des animaux,* the Antwerp French edition of *Fabulen der dieren* (1578). The 125 plates appear in the Latin edition (1579) and in others as late as 1716 and were copied widely for many years—in Philippe Desprez's *Le théâtre des animaux* with 100 facsimile woodcuts (Paris, 1620), *Trésor de fables* with facsimile engravings by Jan L. Krafft (Brussels, 1734), and *Esopi Leben und auserlesene Fabeln*

2.   Marcus Gheeraerts the elder. Edewaerd de Dene, *De warachtighe fabulen der dieren*. Bruges: Pieter de Clerck for M. Gheeraerts, 1567.

(Nuremberg, 1747), for example. Gheeraerts had a modest but definite role in shifting taste in book illustration from aristocratic remoteness to democratic involvement in the immediate scene, as represented by his addition of the fishermen to the traditional Eagle & Snail design (fig. 2).

A remarkable aspect of the seventeenth-century illustration in England is that the chief figures—Francis Cleyn, Wenceslaus Hollar, and Francis Barlow were all etchers, all illustrators of *Aesop's Fables,* and all indebted to Marcus Gheeraerts. Because of the closeness of this relation, all of Gheeraerts's motifs have been included in the Concordance. Thus we have a clear view of the transition between the continental woodcuts of the fifteenth and sixteenth centuries and the etched work of the major illustrators in seventeenth-century England.

Seventeenth-Century English Aesop Illustrators

In the early seventeenth century three illustrated *Aesops* might be mentioned: Henry Peacham's (1639), Gosson and Eglesfield's (1639), and Owsley and Lillicrap's (1654). Peacham's title page said "with pictures," but no copy of the book seems extant. Judged by his emblem book, the main claim of Peacham's fable-book woodcuts would be that they are the first made by a known Englishman. I have not seen a copy of the first edition of *Aesop* put into verse by William Barret—the first verse translation in English, published by Henry Gosson and Francis Eglesfield in 1639—but among the 231 fable illustrations in the 1651 edition must be most of the 113 said to be in the 1639 edition, and the 31 blocks for the Life of Aesop, which follows the fables, are doubtless the original 31. They are all comically inept small copyings, without art or invention. They seem to have been based on Jerome de Marnef's Paris series or perhaps Pieter van der Borcht's parallel series. The illustrations in the edition printed by J. Owsley and P. Lillicrap for Abell Roper (1654) are also insignificant. The blocks seem to have been copied from the Gosson and Eglesfield set and are only a little bit better.

Francis Cleyn (Clein) (1582?–1658), said to be from Rostock, came to England from Denmark in 1625 at the invitation of James I as head of the famous royal tapestry works at Mortlake near Richmond. He also engaged in miscellaneous painting, decorating, and printmaking and made a large number of illustrations, engraved by others, for George Sandys's translation of Ovid's *Metamorphoses* (1632) and John Ogilby's *Virgil* (1654; used later in Dryden's edition). In 1651 he drew and etched the plates for the first edition of Ogilby's *Aesop Paraphras'd*. Though unattractive, they are the first "modern" English *Aesop* series. Their significance here is that, as we shall show in

detail later, they were a bridge between Gheeraerts and
Hollar, between the Continent and England.

Wenceslaus (Wenzel, Václav) Hollar (1607–1677) of
Prague was brought to London by Thomas Howard, first
earl of Arundel, in 1636. He etched hundreds of topographical and architectural prints, copies of paintings, and
title pages with a delicacy of touch and command of
fastidious detail that is often astonishing. Although he
etched other artists' illustrations, principally Cleyn's and
Barlow's, his own memorable interpretive illustrations are
those in the second edition of John Ogilby's *Aesop Paraphras'd* (1665) and in *Aesopics* and *The Ephesian Matron,*
which appeared together with *Aesop Paraphras'd* in
1668.

Francis Barlow (1626?–1704) is best known as the father

3. Francis Barlow. *Aesop's Fables*. London: William Godbid for F.
Barlow, 1666.

4. Engraved by Audinet after Francis Barlow. *Aesop's Fables*. London: John Stockdale, 1793.

of the British sporting print and as the first British bird and animal painter, but he was also the first native-born English etcher of importance and the first major English book illustrator. The 10 etchings he contributed to Edward Benlowe's *Theophila* (1652) are among the most distinguished of interpretive illustrations in any English book. The 110 etched illustrations for his *Aesop* (1666) and the 31 for his Life of Aesop in the second edition (1687) make up one of the most elaborate and delightful series in the whole history of Aesopic fable illustrations. They were admired and copied for generations, as indicated by the faithful reproduction of Barlow's Snake & File in a 1793 engraving (figs. 3, 4).

Here is a remarkable chapter in the history of English book illustration. Ever since Caxton's time English books had been illustrated by anonymous and—with a few exceptions, such as Foxe's *Actes and Monuments* (1563,

1570) and Holinshed's *Chronicles* (1577)—derivative and undistinguished woodcuts. Now in the seventeenth century England joins what we recognize as the Northern European modern tradition of naturalistic book illustration. The fact that Hollar is one of the greatest etchers who ever lived and that Barlow has been called by Otto Benesch (formerly Chief Curator of the Albertina Museum, Vienna) "one of the greatest illustrators of all time" gives weight to any examination of their Aesopic fable designs, their major efforts in book illustration. Because the distinction of the execution of their illustrations is imposed on traditional continental motifs, an account of the transmission of all of their motifs from the original sources in printed books with an analysis of the degree of indebtedness at each step is enlightening in itself and profitable as a modest exercise in art history.

5. Elisha Kirkall. Samuel Croxall, *Fables of Aesop and Others.* London: Jacob Tonson and John Watts, 1722.

6. Thomas Bewick. Samuel Croxall adapted, *The Fables of Aesop and Others*. Newcastle: E. Walter for T. Bewick, 1818.

Notable Later English Editions

This account of Aesopic illustration ends with Barlow, but the traditional designs discussed here continued to be handed down through the eighteenth and nineteenth centuries. Barlow had a strong influence for many years not only in England but throughout Europe. In England tradition carried on into the eighteenth century by way of Elisha Kirkall's borrowing of 85 of Barlow's motifs for the 196 small neat illustrations in the first edition of Samuel Croxall's *Fables of Aesop and Others* (1722), long popular in the United States as well as in England. There now is no doubt that Kirkall drew the designs and engraved them in relief on metal and that he deserves the credit for introducing to England the white-line technique followed by Thomas Bewick. His Birds, Beasts, & Bat (fig. 5) and

Bewick's 1818 Peacocks & Daw (fig. 6) show how they worked from dark to light.

Among the most notable eighteenth-, nineteenth-, and twentieth-century English editions of *Aesop's Fables* are those illustrated by Bewick after Kirkall (Thomas Saint, 1784); various engravers after Barlow (John Stockdale, 1793); Bewick again, also after Kirkall (Thomas Bewick, 1818); an anonymous artist (Charles Whittingham, 1821); James Northcote and William Harvey (G. Lawford, 1828, 1833); Sir John Tenniel (John Murray, 1848); Charles H. Bennett (Kent, 1858); an anonymous artist (Warne, 1866); Joseph Wolf, Johann B. Zwecker, and Thomas Dalziel (A. Strahan, 1867); Harrison Weir (Routledge, 1867); Arthur Rackham (Heinemann, 1912); Agnes Miller Parker (Gregynog, 1931); and Stephen Gooden (Harrap, 1936).

2. The Illustration of *Aesop's Fables*

The Function of Fable Illustration

As we have noted, *Aesop* is one of the few books that with little or no alteration of text have been read by all ages. In general, editors and publishers have distinguished, or have thought they were distinguishing, among readers, but illustrators and readers have been less selective. Many artists have only one style and cannot adjust it for different readers. Others draw to please themselves and consider it improper to take anyone else's reactions into account. In any case, the distinction is no concern of ours. We are looking for excellence wherever we can find it, but at an adult level of interest. Most *Aesops* published nowadays for young children contain illustrations that can be judged only in terms of the needs of young children, a matter outside of our competence. Some of the boringly simple ones may be classics among the five-year-olds, as certainly some of those most admired by adults seem far too sophisticated for young children.

Illustrations by well-known artists have been the main reason for many editions of *Aesop*. But, since animals are the most numerous actors, few artists have equaled Gheeraerts and Barlow in coping with the special problems of drawing them convincingly, often in quite unnatural postures. Animals (a term which here includes birds and mythical creatures) are more interesting to look at than people because they are more symmetrical and graceful than angular, draped human figures, or because we do not see them so much, or, if they are domesticated, because we are more indiscriminately fond of them than we are of our fellow men. To have them caught in predicaments like ours

7. Virgil Solis. *Aesopi Phrygis fabule*. Frankfort: Sigmund Feyerabend, Georg Rab, and
Weigand Han, 1566.

and discuss their problems gives them a fresh interest,
whether or not we are old enough to penetrate, or remem-
ber, the substitution of animals for human beings that
distinguishes Aesopic fables from bestiaries and other
animal stories. Virgil Solis's woodcut of the fox whose
encounters with lions banished its fear of them is the
Aesopic fable illustration in essence (fig. 7).

It may be desirable at this point to clarify some ideas
about fable illustration. Until recently writers about
English book illustration have mostly been print-room
experts, publishers, printers, and artists, persons almost
exclusively concerned with the illustration as an individual
print and with its relation to the type and the appearance of
the book. Book illustration involves other considerations
beyond these, and the illustrations in English fable books
afford a favorable opportunity to explore them. Confusion
also arises from a failure to distinguish between explana-
tory pictures in scientific, travel, and other informational
books on the one hand and imaginative pictures in books of
fiction, poetry, plays, and essays on the other. Confusion
also arises from a failure to distinguish between interpretive
illustrations in a book and frontispieces, title pages, orna-
mental borders, and other decorative designs that may be

present. In a literal sense any picture in any book is illustration, but our discussion relates to the customary meaning of illustration as graphic realization of scenes in works of literature.

The primary function of an illustrator of belles lettres is to represent, interpret, and heighten the meaning of a specific text. His success depends first of all on his intelligence and imagination in understanding the author's intentions, but he can make his understanding manifest only as far as his art reaches. Then he has a secondary function to provide an aesthetic experience different in kind from but complementary to that of the text, like wine with food. These generally accepted premises have in practice often been ignored. The mass of illustrators, including fable illustrators, have been content to "tell the story" in a picture or even merely to show what they imagine the actors might look like.

There remains the readers' response, a subject that has been given little attention. Presumably readers have usually "read" the Aesopic illustration before the text, since it usually dominates the page on which the fable begins. In the past a great many "readers" besides children must have depended on the pictures and hearsay because they were too unlettered to read the words. The completeness and clarity with which a fable can be "told" in one picture varies with the fables. A fox on the ground looking up at a cock in a tree tells only that they are the central characters and that the fable will probably record their dialogue. A fox on the ground looking up at a crow in a tree with food in its mouth tells that the fox wants the food and implies either that he will outwit the crow and get it or that the crow will outwit him and he will do without. The more concretely and uniquely situational the fable, the more intelligibly it can be represented. When seen alone, the most difficult woodcuts to relate to the proper fables are the ones in which animals are shown merely talking to one another. The easiest are those like the Cock & Gem and Snake & Countryman (fig. 8), which cannot well be anything else but what they

8.   Wenceslaus Hollar. John Ogilby, *The Fables of Aesop, Paraphras'd in Verse.* London: Thomas Roycroft for J. Ogilby, 1665.

are. In either case, the first measure of the caliber of the artist as illustrator is whether or not his picture does more than clarify the obvious.

Conditions Attending Early Aesopic Illustration

This inquiry is limited to illustrations in printed books, but of course the motifs of many of the designs appeared as drawings in manuscripts for centuries before printing. The reproductions in Georg Thiele's *Der illustrierte lateinische Aesop,* especially the one of the Wolf & Kid from the tenth- or eleventh-century Leiden Codex Vossianus 15, those of eleventh-, thirteenth-, and fourteenth-century drawings in Julia Bastin's introduction to Dalbanne's facsimiles of the woodcuts in the 1486 Lyons *Aesop,* and those of the illuminations in the thirteenth-century *Ysopet de Lyon* offer random but convincing proof of how early some of the familiar motifs took form. In theory the source of any motif in the Concordance may have been a manuscript drawing, especially in those instances where no source has been found, but it would be farfetched to imagine this in fact true with respect to Gheeraerts or any of the London artists.

Establishing a chain of descent for nearly two hundred illustrations by Gheeraerts, Cleyn, Hollar, and Barlow provides a statistically comprehensive basis for a study of the transmission of secular designs. It also does something toward giving us an understanding of how early artists went about illustrating a standard literary work. Beyond that, however, the many treatments of more or less identical subjects throw some light on questions of borrowing and originality, of changing styles with particular reference to woodcuts and etchings, and even the ultimate question of what constitutes excellence in the illustration of belles lettres.

The elemental incidents dictated the simplified basic compositions of the illuminated manuscripts, and these were followed in the woodcuts of the incunabula. Then all over Europe a body of similar illustrations evolved as artists

and unoriginal craftsmen copied, rearranged, and re-
created these prototypes to fit the fables chosen for reprint-
ing, translation, and rewriting in specific editions. On their
first occurrence newly invented fables of course required
new designs. Later if the text was exceptional, the artist had
to invent, adjust, or follow a particular earlier edition, when
there was one. In some instances, of course, the printer who
controlled a publication was mainly interested in pirating a
popular set of illustrations, often in facsimile. Then the text
might either be borrowed from the same or another source
or written afresh to fit different space requirements or
editorial formulas. The important point is that no necessary
connection exists between the literary sources of Aesopic
fables and the illustrations that accompany them. If the
fable was a simple traditional version, the artist could feel
free to model his designs on any set he fancied or had
available, which might or might not be the edition used by
the printer or editor. This fact can sometimes make serious
discussion of the relation of picture and text pointless.

Woodcuts and Etchings

It seems to have been only by chance that Gheeraerts,
Cleyn, Hollar, and Barlow all used etching rather than
engraving as their medium in illustrating *Aesop*. Without
any doubt Gheeraerts's example inspired the others. Hollar
in exile made copies of Gheeraerts's fable designs and later
copied his "Procession of the Order of the Garter," and he
etched a portrait of Marcus the younger. Gheeraerts seems
not to have known Gabriello Faerno's *Fabulae centum*
(Vincenzio Luchino, Rome, 1536), which contains one of
the rare extensive series of etched book illustrations earlier
than his. They are now attributed to Pirro Ligorio (fig. 9).
Though Aesopic, few of the *Faerno* motifs fall within the
same traditional sequence as Gheeraerts's. Gheeraerts's
decision to turn the traditional woodcut designs into etched
plates meant that the original drawings could be more
realistic in all ways. The craggy Ulm outline woodcuts had

9. Pirro Ligorio. Gabriello Faerno, *Fabule centum*. Rome: Vincenzio Luchino, 1563.

been refined in the small woodcuts of later French editions. But by substituting one freely moving scratch of a needle for two stiff cuts of a knife, Gheeraerts was able to change the nature of the *Aesop* illustration and to contribute to changing the character of European book illustration in

three ways: by the inclusion of an abundance of small
realistic detail, by the expansion of midground and background activity, and by better control of shading to model
form accurately and to simulate the play of light and shade
over an entire scene.

The several *Aesop* series, therefore, afford a perhaps
unique opportunity to compare in depth the differences in
effect of woodcut and etching as media in illustration. The
woodcut, because of its slow and specialized craftsmanship,
more often than not involved a second hand, the
Formschneider, to cut the block after the artist drew a
design on it—that is, if the *Formschneider* did not trace the
drawing or take an impression from a block already cut.
The cutter's aim was facsimile preservation of the lines the
artist drew, but the character of a pen or pencil line
inevitably changes when reproduced in wood and by cutters
of varying skills. The nature of etching makes it natural,
although not necessary, for the artist to draw the design
with a needle on the plate, apply the acid, and pull the
proofs himself. In the English series several designs are
reproduced by burin engraving, which also normally introduces a second hand. The burin was freely used by early
etchers, and etching by engravers, so that it is sometimes
difficult to say which technique is dominant. In the editions
that mainly concern us, however, the identity of the artists
and their media are certain with only a few exceptions.
Copying of etched illustrations is much more difficult than
copying of woodcuts. A facsimile of a woodcut illustration
can be made by any highly skilled cutter; only a talented
artist-etcher can come close to duplicating an etched series,
as Gilles Sadeler did in his *Theatrum morum* (Prague,
1609) copies of Gheeraerts's 1578 *Aesop* series.

3. Motifs, Transmission, and Indebtedness

Defining the Motif

Fables are short, and in most illustrated editions each fable has its own picture—and only one. The shortness normally reduces the action to one or the other of two possibilities: A meets B and they talk; or, A meets B and one thing happens. Either way, A or B, whichever is the mouthpiece for Aesop, makes a wise, or worldly-wise, comment, which is never illustrated. This concentration of event keeps the motif of an Aesopic illustration within an extremely narrow conceptual range. To illustrate the fable of the Wolf & Crane, the artist really has no option but to show the crane at some point in the act of removing the obstruction from the wolf's throat, and the two creatures must be facing one another, with the wolf usually seated and with his head raised, as in Barlow's naturalistic version (fig. 10). This elemental concept, embodied in the earliest manuscript illustrations, is what all illustrators of the traditional, unelaborated fable have begun with. Even here, however, basic visualizations can vary in a limited way—the head of the crane, for example, can be inside the wolf's mouth entirely, partly, or not at all. In the fable of the fox that escapes from a well by stepping on the head of the goat he has lured in after him, the fox can be shown either as jumping out or, having escaped, as peering in at the goat. These are different motifs. In the design for the Wolf & Crane, so long as they retain their customary posture, the position of the crane's head, though critical, is only a variable detail.

Motif as used here designates the ideographic pattern made by the posture and relation to one another of the main characters (and sometimes an object) as they act out the

10.   Francis Barlow. *Aesop's Fables*. London: William Godbid for F. Barlow, 1666.

fable situation, often at its climax. At times in this study when the context seems to make the substitution clear, the word *concept* may be used instead of the word *motif*. The word *design* refers to the finished illustration. The word *motif* is, of course, often used by others in a narrower sense, as a repeated theme or unit in a single work, for example, in a piece of music or in a pattern for textiles. In an illustration for the fable of the lion's share, for instance, a lion wearing a crown may conceivably be thought of as a motif; in this study, however, the posture of the lion and his relation to the other animals is what is meant by the word *motif*. Whether the lion wears a crown or not is an incidental variable, although it might be evidence of borrowing. Again, motif and composition are virtually identical in the early woodcuts, but newly introduced

objects may play an important structural role in an individual composition without altering the basic motif. These
remarks are merely an explanation of the usage of terms in
this study, not dogma. The terms are important, however,
because it is easy to talk nonsense about the relation
between illustrations by concentrating on details without
comparing or even recognizing the motifs.

The Artist's Freedom

The brevity of the fable text eliminates description, emotive
imagery, author's analysis, and other obstacles to illustrators. These conditions, taken together with wide familiarity
with the fables as stories and as a literary form, have offered
illustrators a unique freedom. The Aesopic fable frees the
illustrator from domination by the text, so much resented by
contemporary artists. So long as he shows a wolf and a
crane in revelatory action, the illustrator can draw them as
wild creatures in the depths of a forest or outside a rural
village, or as dressed in the human fashions of the day in a
contemporary dining room, or as whatever his imagination
suggests.

Paradoxically, however, this freedom was restricted by
the early illustrators themselves. For three centuries,
respect for the traditional, zeal to cash in on others' success,
and lack of time, craft, or imagination produced a great deal
of mechanical copying. During these centuries only the
major illustrators accepted the traditional motifs and still
overlaid them with their own fresh vision of what the scene
was like as it appeared on the screen of their imagination.
In the last two centuries, it is true, fear of the charge of
plagiarism has led artists to make self-conscious efforts to be
different; and yet time after time the bare-bones structure of
the fable forces them back to traditional motifs. What the
individual artist does with his limited options is what
determines how good an illustrator he is.

The fable-book illustrator has almost always silently
claimed one freedom: he has made no effort to communicate

the meaning of the fable—its moral, lesson, or application, as it has been variously called. In the sixteenth century some emblem-book material, together with the illustrations, entered fable books, and illustrators perpetuated emblematic designs. But the fable writers chose adaptable situational material; they rarely entered into the emblem-book game of extracting allegorical meanings from abstract symbolic devices. The morals and applications drawn by successive editors of English fable books, often at twice the length of the fables themselves, have been wise and eccentric, pious and cynical, but they have rarely directly affected the illustrations. Of course, the assignment of symbolic characteristics to animals is older than the fables themselves. Even today children are probably aware that the fox is clever, the wolf savage, and the lion regal, but they do not go beyond such simplifications. English illustrators have sometimes stressed these roles, but more often they have simply tried faithfully to draw animals in the condition indicated, such as a lion that is sick or a dog that is angry. This lack of commitment to the didactic purpose of the fables may account for much of the appeal of Aesopic illustrations to ordinary readers and thus of the fable books themselves.

Transmission of Motifs

The early illustrators of *Aesop,* as we have said, were content to repeat the motifs of one or more earlier series, with such practical adjustments as were forced on them and such embellishments as pleased them. Thus the motifs in many continental fable illustrations go back to manuscript illuminations and to the early series printed in Bamberg and Ulm, Lyons, and Venice. The effects vary with local styles and with the capabilities of the artists and woodcutters; yet for the main body of fable illustrations from Albrecht Pfister of Bamberg to Barlow a continuity of motifs is clearly traceable. The nature of the early fable, with its single-episode construction and unambiguous climax, makes some similarity in graphic representation

inevitable. After 1700 new social outlooks, more individual-
istic authors, newly invented fables, more particularization
of texts, topical applications, and growing self-conscious-
ness among artists about plagiarism and originality
dispersed this uniformity. The old motifs persisted,
nevertheless, well into the twentieth century, mainly in
children's editions.

Indebtedness in book illustration before 1700 is not so
easy to specify as the use of the term and the symbols in the
Concordance may suggest. In the first place, the notion of
plagiarism had not yet occurred to artists, or at least had
little force among them; therefore much of the continuity
derives from overt borrowing. This varies, however, from
the nearly photographic facsimile copies of Bernard Salomon's designs made for de Marnef to Barlow's re-creations.
The degree of indebtedness also varies among sources and
within single series. Sometimes artists followed their models
with little or no change of the basic action. Sometimes they
reproduced the essential features faithfully and varied
details—except in facsimile copies almost always they
changed dress and background. Sometimes they studied a
design but did it over freely with additions and subtractions,
occasionally to fit deviations in their text, more often to no
apparent purpose. Sometimes they combined elements from
more than one model. Sometimes they either invented new
designs or else borrowed to an unimaginable degree from
sources not known or not recognized in this study. And, of
course, designs adjust to changes in the shape and size of
printed pages, technical media, and artistic fashions. Thus,
although the source of the illustrations in an edition
sometimes can be assigned with certainty, the determination
is often subject to varying degrees of probability.

Determination of borrowing among *Aesop* illustrators
before 1700, when motifs were common property, calls for
close observation of correspondences and variations not only
in specific designs but throughout entire series, for acquain-
tance with other illustrated editions in the period, and for a
sharp awareness of the styles and habits of artists whose
work is being compared. In the instance of the Lion &

Mouse illustrations in the Bamberg and Ulm editions, with the mouse gnawing a rope toward the top of a pole, it seems clear that Zainer's design was borrowed from Pfister's as soon as it is seen that later motifs show the lion caught in a net (see pls. 22–30). This conclusion, questionable in relation to only one design, becomes an acceptable probability in the light of the large number of similar correspondences between the two editions and the state of German printing in the 1460s and '70s, including its geography. Bamberg, Ulm, Augsburg, and Nuremberg are not far apart. That Gheeraerts in 1567 would borrow substantially from Christopher Plantin's 1565 *Aesop* facsimile copies of Bernard Saloman's designs rather than from Solis's 1566 copies seems logical because Solis's *Aesop* was published only in the year before Gheeraerts's *Fabulen der dieren* and contains a great many fables and illustrations not in the Bruges collection. This false impression changes only when the facts are finally sorted out. In spite of obvious similarities, Cleyn seemed not to have borrowed from Gheeraerts or Hollar from Cleyn when several years ago I first compared their editions, because my concept of borrowing was then too narrow. The truth became clear only after I acquired a better understanding of *Aesop* borrowing in general and of the specific habits of Cleyn and Hollar.

Side-by-side study of all the designs in related editions over a period of weeks and months, discontinued, and then done all over again several times gradually brings insight into the nature of the whole problem. From this insight, with details seen in perspective, emerge judgments that often reverse early ones. They are sometimes difficult to put into words convincingly, let alone into symbols. They are the opposite of intuitional, however, because they are the product of the accumulation and synthesis of masses of data, observations, and impressions.

Determining Degrees of Indebtedness

It is not possible to classify all variation in indebtedness with anything like Linnaean consistency, except in instances of facsimile copying—which, however, does not occur in the illustrations of Gheeraerts and the artists in England. Only design-by-design comparison can reveal how, as in a hundred paintings of the Annunciation, similar illustrations can vary in degrees of originality, so that on occasion the execution of a borrowed motif, the important element in all Aesopic borrowing, can be artistically superior to its source and even more "original." The line of descent is not an unbroken one; different choices of fables by some editors and translators and invention of new fables by others make this impossible. An artist may depend on one edition for his main inspiration and yet have to borrow from another source or invent fresh designs for one or more fables.

Two points in the preceding paragraph are crucial in this study and might be clarified by examples. First, take the statement that the motif—the posture and arrangement of the fable characters in acting out the basic idea of the illustration—is what is important in borrowing. In a cursory inspection Denys Janot's design for Juno, Peacock, & Nightingale bears little resemblance to Zainer's. It is not even in the same order. But this initial difference is meaningless; one woodcut design drawn from another must print in reverse unless it is turned over before being transferred to the block. Other differences may seem more important. In Zainer's version for instance, Juno is naked except for a turban, the peacock has a long sweeping tail, and a shield hangs on a tree. In Janot's design Juno wears a gown and crown, the peacock's tail is spread and lifted, and no shield appears. What points to borrowing is the fact that in both illustrations, in the same triangular pattern, Juno holding a scepter stands facing a peacock, while a smaller bird sits on the branch of a tree. The close resemblance of the two nightingales, their perch, and their position in the triangle is significant. It is the kind of unobtrusive element a borrower does not trouble to alter. Salomon later rearranged this motif by one key change: he elevated Juno to a cloud. Thereafter other artists in the Hollar-Barlow sequence changed details, but they kept Juno aloft. The

11. Wenceslaus Hollar. John Ogilby, *The Fables of Aesop, Paraphras'd in Verse*. London: Thomas Roycroft for J. Ogilby, 1665.

motif embodying the essential concept of an illustration is
what is borrowed, but there is no mechanical way to assess
the evidence that borrowing has taken place, especially
without supporting evidence independent of two designs.

    That a borrowed design can seem more original than its

source is even less easily demonstrated. Early illustrations of the fable of the dialogue between a mother crab and her young one, for instance, show two crayfish lying parallel on a river bank until Gheeraerts imagined them as small round shellfish swimming in a river. Hollar could not very well invent a new basic concept, but he gave a completely fresh impression to the old one by etching two beautifully detailed crabs, a mother and a young one, at right angles to one another with their claws entwined (fig. 11). They seem huge and important because Hollar has shown them close-up, lying on a dune overlooking an ocean harbor in which ships, fishermen, sailors, and strollers on the beach are tiny and remote. This is one of the difficult conversational fables. The Eagle & Fox is one of the situational fables. Pfister, precisely copied by Zainer, piled some neatly bound sheaves of grain at the foot of the eagle's eyrie for the

12.   Francis Barlow. *Aesop's Fables*. London: William Godbid for F. Barlow, 1666.

fox to set fire. All the artists except Barlow showed the
vixen with the flaming brand in her mouth and standing on
the ground. Barlow moved her up onto a branch directly
under the nest. Thus he had room for a drawing of a
majestic eagle with its young and the fox pup that fills the
breadth of the rectangular plate, while the vixen close below
is so convincing that the improbability of the action is
forgotten (fig. 12). In this instance the originality lies first
in the imaginative reconstruction of the situation and then
in the quality of the drawing and the etching which give the
motif artistic form. For Ogilby's 1668 *Aesopics* Barlow
redrew this design, but it loses its special force on a tall plate
in the less sensitive etching of Richard Gaywood.

Aim of This Study

An analysis of the descent of the traditional *Aesop* motifs
from which English illustrators' designs evolve promises to
lead to a better understanding not only of their work but
also of the beginnings of modern English book illustration
in the seventeenth century. At the same time, the study aims
in an unpretentious way to subject one phase of English
book illustration to something of the discipline of other
bibliographical studies. The Aesopic fable illustrations are
ideal for such an investigation because of the continuity of
their motifs from the first printed edition to Barlow's
edition. The key questions requiring answers are: (*a*) What
are the sources used by each artist in this sequence? (*b*)
What is the degree of his indebtedness to his sources? The
inquiry widens rapidly. A general pattern of descent
emerges, but individual designs often have exceptional
histories.

To give a full account of the transmission process by
which the traditional motifs were incorporated in the art of
Hollar and Barlow, the inquiry must, as we have said,
include the Aesopic illustrations of Marcus Gheeraerts the
elder and Francis Cleyn. Gheeraerts was the primary
source for both Cleyn and Barlow, and though the first

edition of his fable book was published in Bruges, he came to England and is the first identifiable artist to do any significant book illustrating in England. Cleyn was the primary source for Hollar. His *Ovid, Aesop,* and *Virgil* illustrations are not appealing, but the quantity of them makes him the first known illustrator of consequence in England after Gheeraerts. With all of Gheeraerts's and Cleyn's *Aesop* illustrations included in the Concordance, we have a clear and unambiguous view of the transition between the continental designs of the fifteenth and sixteenth centuries and the designs of Hollar and Barlow in seventeenth-century England.

In order to account for the sources and transmission of all of the 199 Aesop illustrations of these four artists, it has been necessary to go back to the beginning of the tradition of the illustration of Aesopic fables in printed books. It should be understood, however, that the illustrations in these earlier editions are outside the area of main interest of this study; comments on them here may be considered suggestions for further investigation by anyone interested. It should also be remembered that we are tracing only our 199 designs, and these only in what we consider the key editions for the transmission of the motifs that appear in the illustrations of Gheeraerts and the chief seventeenth-century English artists. We are ignoring other Aesopic illustrations and editions of equal importance for similar inquiries about continental sequences.

4. Continental Sources of English *Aesop* Motifs

The hundreds of illustrated editions of Aesopic fables printed before 1700, each with scores of cuts, make the search for borrowings hazardous and dogmatic attributions reckless. The British Library collection of printed *Aesop*s is one of the world's most comprehensive, but it has gaps. Nevertheless, with help from the Victoria and Albert Museum and Bodleian Library collections, from xerographic copies, and from the writings of scholars who have dealt with specific aspects of the history of Aesopic fables, it has been possible to trace with reasonable reliability the probable relations among the editions of fable and emblem books that served as sources for motifs in seventeenth-century English illustrations.

At this point, a summary list of the sources should make the detailed account that follows easier to understand. Aptly enough, the wellspring of this tradition is the first dated illustrated book, Ulrich Boner's *Der Edelstein*, a collection of Aesopic fables printed by Albrecht Pfister in Bamberg, 1461. Next is the famous *Aesop* of Johann Zainer, printer of Ulm (ca. 1476), which is often mistakenly considered the first printed fable book. After Pfister and Zainer the simplified line of descent seems the following (to use the short identification adopted in the Concordance): Sebastian Brant (Basel, 1501); Denys Janot (Paris, 1542); Bernard Salomon (Lyons, 1547, etc.); Christopher Plantin (Antwerp, 1565); Virgil Solis (Frankfort, 1566); Marcus Gheeraerts (Bruges, 1567, and Antwerp, 1578); Francis Cleyn (1651); Wenceslaus Hollar and "Roderigo" (Dirk) Stoop (1665); Francis Barlow (1666); Hollar and Barlow (1668). After Gheeraerts the place of printing is London (see Chart, p. 73).

The Life of Aesop illustrations came down separately from Zainer to Jerome de Marnef (Paris, 1582), probably by an intermediate stage, to Pieter van der Borcht, artist for Jan Mourentorf, printer (Antwerp, 1593), or a closely similar edition, and then to Barlow (1687). Since Gheeraerts, Cleyn, and Hollar did not illustrate the Life, Barlow's set stands apart from our inquiry and is not listed in the Concordance.

As emblem books became fashionable in the sixteenth century, fable books enjoyed an infusion of emblematic elements. Yet few motifs used after Gheeraerts are originally emblem-book devices. The sequence of editions of Andrea Alciati's *Emblematum liber*, which are the main sources for fable-book use of emblem-book devices, in summary by printers seems the following: Heinrich Steyner (Augsburg, 1531, the *editio princeps*); Chrestien Wechel (Paris, 1534); Jean de Tournes and Guillaume Gazeau (Lyons, 1547); and Christopher Plantin (Antwerp, 1565, etc.).

Now let us examine all of these continental fable-book and emblem-book sources one by one.

Albrecht Pfister of Bamberg (1461)

The corpus of *Aesop* illustrations in printed books begins with the first dated illustrated book, printed by Albrecht Pfister at Bamberg in 1461. It is Ulrich Boner's *Der Edelstein*, a fourteenth-century collection of 100 verse fables from Avianus and other sources. Motifs for 51 of the 103 *Edelstein* outline woodcuts (ca. 77 × 105 mm.) are listed later in the Concordance (see pls. 22, 31). The designs are primitive and technically simple, but they seem the most expressive and delightful of all fable illustrations in Northern European incunabula. The artist tailored the design to the psychological event as it affected him. Thus, for example, in the fable of the Wolf, Child, & Nurse, the wolf is a fearsome beast with a long neck and conspicuous claws, and he is almost as high as the abstraction of a house

in which, framed in a window out of all scale with the
building, the nurse clutches a baby in her arms. In the fable
of the Ox & Frog, the two frogs confronting an ox are as
large as the ox's head and have a neatly stylized double row
of circles like buttons down their backs. The Bamberg
illustrator lacked the art of the Italian woodcut designers in
managing space relations, and some of his quaintness comes
from anatomical ambiguity. But he evoked the essential
situation of each of Boner's versified fables with great
economy of lines cut with fearless slices of the knife. Much
of the expressiveness is due to this bold cutting, which in
this instance is not unlikely to have been by the same hand
that drew the designs.

It would be gratifying to bestow on the anonymous
illustrator of these first imaginative fable designs the title of
"Bamberg Master," but clearly he was closely dependent
on the drawings in one of the manuscripts of *Der Edelstein*.
Dr. Doris Fouquet of the Herzog August Bibliothek at
Wolfenbüttel—editor of a facsimile edition of the Wolfenbüttel example of Pfister's book, one of the two extant—
agrees but says in a letter that she has not found the source,
though she has seen almost all of the dozen extant manuscripts. The style of the woodcuts is unmistakably similar to
that of reproductions from three of the manuscripts of
different times, but the woodcuts are superior as works of
art.

Little serious critical recognition has been given the
Edelstein illustrations. William Morris called the Zainer
Aesop "incomparably the best and most expressive of the
many illustrated editions of the Fables printed in the
fifteenth century," but it is hardly possible that he ever saw
a copy of *Der Edelstein*. In his introduction to a facsimile
edition of the Berlin undated *Edelstein* and in *Kupferstich
und Holzschnitt in vier Jahrhunderten*, Paul O. Kristeller
does not discuss the merits of the woodcuts and does not
compare them with Zainer's. Wilhelm Worringer in *Die
altdeutsche Buchillustration* praises the Ulm *Aesop* but in
his discussion of Pfister fails to mention *Der Edelstein*.

A.W. Pollard gives short shrift to the *Edelstein* illustrations in *Early Illustrated Books*. He lumps them with the rest of Pfister's woodcuts as "executed in clumsy outline." A.M. Hind knew *Der Edelstein* but seems not to have looked at reproductions of the woodcuts more than casually, for he makes only noncommittal references to them and calls Zainer's the work of "the *Aesop* master." Even as late as 1964 Ferdinand Geldner, in *Die Buchdruckerkunst im alten Bamberg 1458/59 bis 1519*, bows to Zainer's woodcuts as far superior to Pfister's. This certainty remains unchallenged in later works by Geldner, Maria Lanckorońska, Herbert C. Schulz, and Ernst Weil. Kristeller's guess that the printer Pfister was his own artist and woodcutter overlooks the fact that his *Edelstein* and *Ackermann von Böhmen* are by different hands.

William M. Ivins, Jr., in *The Artist and the Fifteenth-Century Printer* offers the following curious sociological explanation for what he seems to have considered the self-evident superiority of Zainer's woodcuts: "Bamberg, where the first illustrated books were produced . . . was not a cultural center . . . in fact, it was a very small provincial town, and its book illustrations quite naturally rough, clumsy, uncouth, the work of men but little removed from the yokel, examples not so much of a new art as of the utter degradation of an old one. . . . Ulm and Augsburg were probably among the most highly civilized spots in the Germany of that period. . . . Such books as the Ulm Boccaccio and the Augsburg *Speculum* when compared with the Bamberg *Edelstein* are the work of cultured people." Ironically Schulz believes that the blocks for Pfister's four illustrated books were prepared in Nuremberg.

In "Ulrich Boner's *Edelstein*" Hans Strahm reproduces the nine illuminations in the Berne Municipal Library manuscript (Erlach, between 1466–73). He speaks of their "powerful natural artistry" and says: "The figures are not naturalistic transcriptions of reality, but types eloquent of the characters they embody. They express everything that

requires to be said to the observer or listener through the
picture to ensure that what he has [seen] or heard remains
imprinted on his memory." Pfister's woodcuts are done in
the same spirit and merit the same praise. Quite apart from
the fact that his motifs seem to have been the source for half
of the later Ulm series, Pfister's woodcuts fulfill their
function as illustrations triumphantly, with charm, spirit,
unselfconsciousness, and expressiveness. Some eminent
experts seem to have been beguiled by the superior representation in the Ulm illustrations to prefer them to the
fresh, zestful Bamberg woodcuts.

Johann Zainer of Ulm (ca. 1476)

Zainer's *Aesop* woodcuts (ca. 77 × 105 mm.) appear in the
Concordance 100 times (see pls. 6, 14, 23, 32, 43). Over half
of them (54) are the first occurrences in a printed book and
are therefore either original or derivations from manuscripts such as the eleventh-century Ademar manuscript.
For the rest the degree of probable indebtedness of Zainer's
hand to Pfister's varies a good deal from one woodcut to
another, but there seems no doubt about its actuality. The
Ulm series includes 46 of the 51 Bamberg motifs that are
listed in the Concordance, and 19 seem close to identical. In
addition it has a Life of Aesop series not present in *Der
Edelstein*. The proof that Zainer's hand did in fact use
Pfister's woodcuts is available: Pfister's man made the error
of cutting a lion to represent *De apro*, and Zainer's man
followed him. Sebastian Brant, a better Latinist, had a new
block of a boar cut for this fable of the Ass & Boar when in
1501 he reprinted Zainer's edition with facsimiles of the
woodcuts and had a new hand illustrate his own added
fables.

Zainer's hand traced none of the *Edelstein* motifs. The
variations between his blocks and the 46 parallel ones in the
Edelstein set can be attributed either to a moderate asser-
tion of individuality, conformity to the new style, or use of
similar but different sources, possibly the same manuscript

or manuscripts on which he based his 54 first printed-book occurrences and his Life of Aesop series. In the face of so much correspondence with the *Edelstein* motifs, it is too much to imagine that he invented completely fresh designs for the fables not in *Der Edelstein*. Lanckorońska suggests that Matthaus Neithart, a sculptor, drew Zainer's designs. Without proof that Zainer's hand used manuscript sources for the 46 fables illustrated in common with Pfister's, it seems logical to think he found stimulation and convenient models in the novel woodcut illustrations in *Der Edelstein*.

The Zainer woodcuts are naturalistic only in comparison with the Pfister blocks. They also are restricted to the chief actors, minimum accessories, bumpy terrain, and a tree or two as in the cut of the Fox & Crane (fig. 13). The naturalism is largely one of intent. The *Edelstein* tree foliage is a cluster of symbolic blades; the Ulm foliage of flying parentheses fails to represent leaves realistically or to

13. Anonymous. *Vita Esopi et fabule.* Heinrich Steinhöwel, tr. Augsburg: Anton Sorg, [1480?]. From Johann Zainer, Ulm, [ca. 1476].

suggest them interestingly. The halfhearted shading seems
an effort to reproduce the modeling of a manuscript wash
tint or of hand-colored *Edelstein* woodcuts. The gnarled
Gothic outline and the obstinate angularity of drapery folds,
so compelling in the woodcuts of Dürer and other German
masters, here lose the authority of original drawing and
take on the calculation of imitation. It is also apparent that
the draftsman sought merely to get his figures on the block
without much thought about compositional niceties. But
Zainer's woodcuts and their copies pleased generations of
readers in several countries. They were part of the *Aesop*
reading experience, and they fulfilled their narrative function admirably.

Sebastian Brant of Basel (1501)

An interesting but uncertain intermediate *Aesop* is the one
printed at Basel by Jacob Wolff of Pfortzheim in 1501. It is
really two separate works bound together. The first part
pirates Zainer's woodcut series for the Life of Aesop and
the fables, such as the Ant & Fly (fig. 14), with 3 by the
hand that cut the blocks for the second part. Part two is a
new collection of Aesopic fables prepared by the satirical
humanist Sebastian Brant. Because this second part
contains motifs that seem to have been the first to precede
several of Denys Janot's designs, we shall refer to the
edition as Brant's, rather than as that of Wolff or the
"Master of the Grüninger office," who is supposed to have
prepared the woodcuts of the second part from sketches by
Brant and with his advice.

Of the 12 Basel 1501 designs listed among the motifs in
the Concordance, 11 have their origin in these new cuts (79
X 115 mm.) for Brant's fables. Yet even in those several
instances where Brant's motifs from his fables are the only
predecessors of Janot's listed, it is not possible to say that
they are themselves Janot's models. Even so, it seems
desirable to include the dozen Brant illustrations. Whether
or not they are a direct Janot source, they throw light on the

14. Anonymous. *Esopi appologi*. With additions by Sebastian Brant. Basel: Jacob Wolff, 1501.

transition between Zainer and Janot—between Germany and France in a sense—including the adaptation of two of Brant's fable motifs as emblem-book devices.

Emblem Books

As we have observed, emblem-book devices are a secondary source of motifs for illustrations in fable books included in the Concordance. Of the 98 motifs in the first edition of Andrea Alciati's *Emblematum liber*, printed by Heinrich Steyner (Augsburg, 1531), 11 were soon absorbed into the Aesopic fable tradition being traced here, and 3 enter later through subsequent editions. They come to Gheeraerts by way of Chrestien Wechel (Paris, 1534); Jean de Tournes and Guillaume Gazeau with woodcuts by Bernard Salomon (Lyons, 1547); and Christopher Plantin (Antwerp, 1565, 25 October 1566, and 1567). In 2 instances the source seems to be the series in the *Alciati* printed in Lyons by Macé

Bonhomme for Guillaume Rouille (Rouillé, Roville) (1548, etc.) with copies of Salomon's designs by Pierre Eskrich (Cruche or Vase). Plantin may also be the source for 2 other emblematic motifs, one from Claude Paradin's *Heroica* (1562) and just possibly one from Ioannis Sambucus's *Emblemata* (1564).

The emblem devices selected, such as those for the Ass & Thistle (see pls. 1–5), Dolphin & Tuna, Cupid & Death, and Snake & Archer (see pls. 39–42), are the realistic sort easily assimilated as fable illustrations. In fact, 3 of the motifs served in *Aesops* before being adopted by Alciati, one in Pfister's edition and two in Brant's.

In 1567 Sigmund Feyerabend of Frankfort printed two editions of *Alciati*, one Latin and German and the other Latin. The copy of the Latin edition in the British Library has ca. 125 woodcut devices (53 × 67 mm.) in the Solis manner. (Two smaller ones with Solis's monogram are from his 1566 *Aesop*.) They are derived from Salomon and other sources. This edition has not been entered in the Concordance because I have no evidence that it was a source for our later artists. Barlow, however, might have known it and used it for his much altered designs, particularly for his Snake & Fowler, which he evolved from the Snake & Archer motif.

Denys Janot of Paris (1542)

The unknown artist who supplied the Italianate designs for Denys Janot's *Les fables du tresancien Esope, Phrygien* (1542), with text by Gilles Corrozet, is a significant figure in the history of Aesopic fable illustration in Northern Europe. He seems to have been the man who shifted the style from the factual statements of the relatively large German *Aesop* blocks to the sophistications of the small French ones (see pls. 7, 15, 24, 33, 44). He was clearly influenced by Italian reconstructions of Zainer motifs. He could have been an Italian himself or a former associate of Geoffroy Tory, who had earlier introduced the Italian style into French books. In the list of northern book illustrators he is only a few years later than Hans Sebald Beham, Hans Holbein, and Tory, and he is a forerunner of Jost Amman, Salomon, and Solis. If he did not cut his own blocks, he had the services of a good cutter.

The sources of Janot's motifs are not yet certain. David Du Vivier, who is making a study of the Italianate element in French book illustration of this period, states that in his opinion the first 42 of Janot's 100 illustrations (ca. 32 × 57 mm.) are based on an as yet unidentified Venetian series, perhaps 12 or so are based on the illustrations painted over woodcuts in the Bibliothèque Nationale vellum example of Antoine Vérard's edition of Lorenzo Valla's collection of fables (Paris, 1498), 2 blocks derive from Corrozet's *Hecatomgraphie* (Janot, 1540), and 44 derive from as yet unidentified sources. By my own handicapped count, of the 89 Janot motifs in the Concordance 37 seem original or from a source that I have not seen, 46 seem ultimately from Zainer, 1 from Steyner's *Alciati* (1531), 1 from Janot's *Théâtre des bons engins* (1539?) of Guillaume de la Perrière, and 1 conceivably from Pfister. Then 3 motifs seem to derive from Sebastian Brant's two-part edition of Aesopic fables (Basel, 1501), with his additions to Steinhöwel's collection for Zainer. In the first part the design of the Ass & Boar that Brant corrected has no certainty about it, but it is listed as a possibility. The second part contains several designs that resemble Janot's. Only two seem sufficiently similar to be listed with queries. Almost certainly Janot's sources also included some of the illustrations in manuscripts used by Corrozet. For our purposes, however, it is not so important to pinpoint Janot's sources as it is to record that his *Aesop* is the principal source for Bernard Salomon.

Janot's illustrations refine the treatment of Germanic fable motifs. Within small blocks his designer/woodcutter introduced a far greater sense of space by moving the figures back and making them part of a landscape with a distant horizon. In these illustrations the shading is restrained, the line fluent, and the cutting delicate. Direct Italian influence appears in the conscious selection and arrangement of elements for compostional balance and then in the way they are tied together by rhythmic lines. The handsome architectural frame that encloses each woodcut and fable, together with the brevity of the text, reveals the combined influence of Tory and the emblem books of the preceding decade. Since, however, only the slightest evidence suggests that any of the four later artists we are primarily concerned with knew Janot's series, he is for us only transitional, a baiting post on the transmission route.

Bernard Salomon of Lyons (1547)

Historically, Janot's *Aesop* illustrations take precedence over Bernard Salomon's, but Salomon's have been much more popular and have had much more influence (see pls. 8, 16, 25, 34, 45). But since Salomon based his woodcuts for de Tournes's editions of *Aesop* mainly on Janot's, anyone borrowing from Salomon was indebted to Janot's anonymous Paris artist, too. Except for the awkwardness of the reference, these cuts might be called the Janot-Salomon series. But then, too, Salomon and apparently another hand added to the collection after 1547. In any case, because of Salomon's variations the indebtedness to Janot would not be absolute to the degree that anyone following Gerard Leeu's series (Gouda, 1484), say, would be indebted to Zainer or that anyone copying de Marnef's, Plantin's, or Solis's blocks would be indebted to Salomon.

Neither the British Library nor the Victoria and Albert Museum has Salomon's 1547 or 1556 *Aesop*. Therefore I have used the illustrations in his 1551, 1564, and 1570 editions and in de Marnef's 1561 exact facsimiles to predicate Salomon's position in the transmission of motifs. The stratagem seems adequate to establish the chain of descent by series, not by editions, but occasionally the facts may not fit into this Euclidean scheme. Granting that I have made some errors in attributions, I believe that Salomon based 77 of his 106 motifs (ca. 35 × 47 mm.) in the Concordance on Janot, 4 on Zainer, and 10 on Wechel's *Alciati*. Twelve of his *Aesop* designs and 3 of his designs for de Tournes's *Alciati* (1547) seem original or derived from sources not noted. Not counted are 3 instances of designs closely similar to Janot's in de Marnef's edition, which otherwise used facsimiles of Salomon's series. This suggests the probability that 3 transitional Salomon blocks are missing from the editons I have used. In the "Comprehensive Survey of Greek and Latin Fables in the Aesopic Tradition" of his authoritative *Babrius and Phaedrus*, B.E. Perry makes reference to fables for 2 of the 12 designs listed here as original or from undisclosed sources. The early manuscript existence of these two fables introduces the presumption of earlier illustrations that Salomon may have used as sources.

Salomon's borrowing from Janot varies. A good deal of the time he reproduced somewhat more interesting landscape and secondary elements such as buildings, more accurately realized detail, and more color and modeling through shading as in the Snake & Birdcatcher (fig. 15). Superficially, his progress seems toward greater realism, but it is really toward more Italian Mannerist effects. His linear devices are more artful than Janot's—the curves of human and animal figures, trees, terrain, and clouds complement one another prettily, and elongated human figures twist and bend and gesture to create graceful patterns. Salomon's fashionable refinement was reinforced by the desire to harmonize with the new light roman,

15.   Bernard Salomon. *Les fables d'Esope Phrygian*. Lyons: Jean de Tournes and Guillaume Gazeau, 1551.

Greek, and Civilité types that de Tournes used in his popular little editions.

Salomon was fortunate to have his complex little drawings reproduced in wood so well. Many blocks are gems, but a number seem to blur from the difficulty of cutting so much fine detail in so little space. Salomon and what seems his best cutter achieved far better results elsewhere when de Tournes gave them larger blocks to work on. Still, the whole effort to refine the black woodcut line until it reaches the fluency of quill or pencil drawing or burin engraving seems misguided.

Christopher Plantin of Antwerp (1565)

In spite of the disturbed times in which Christopher Plantin worked, some of his illustrated books are among the finest. He had able artists such as Geoffroy Ballain of Paris and Pieter van der Borcht at his disposal, and, though the woodcut era was drawing to a close, Arnold Nicolai, Gerard van Kampen, and other highly skilled woodcutters turned out large numbers of blocks for him. Unfortunately, Plantin's *Aesop* (1565) is not one of his more admirable productions. All but 6 of the 76 woodcut illustrations (ca. 35 × 47 mm.) are traced copies of Salomon's *Aesop* designs. Of the 6, 2 are somewhat larger (55 × 55 mm.). One is a crocodile signed with Gerard van Kampen's "G," and the other, unsigned, is from Plantin's *Sambucus* series. The other 4 are from his *Alciati*. Dr. L. Voet, Director of the Museum Plantin-Moretus, writes about the remaining 70 unsigned Salomon copies: "These illustrations were purchased or borrowed by Plantin from his Antwerp colleague, Jan van Waesberghen." This was not abnormal practice on Plantin's part. Apart from whether or not Plantin's *Aesop* illustrations influenced Gheeraerts or any English illustrators, the book is included in the Concordance because its date and Plantin's prominence ensure that it almost certainly had some part in the transmission of Salomon's versions of traditional motifs.

Virgil Solis of Frankfort (1566)

Virgil Solis extends the Tory-Janot-Salomon Italianate influence to Germany (see pls. 9, 17, 26, 46). Although a painter, engraver, and etcher, his 300 or 400 woodcut illustration are, like Salomon's, for the Bible, Ovid's *Metamorphoses*, and *Aesop*. Because of the charm and easy competence of his woodcuts, we should expect Solis to have a significant part among *Aesop* illustrators. In fact, his role is passive, completely uncreative conceptually or stylistically. Of the 106 of his Frankfort woodcuts (ca. 48 × 67 mm.) listed in the Concordance, all but a few are straightforward reproductions from his sources. Only one seems original or from a source not noted, probably the latter since the fable is recorded by Perry. Solis's main source is Bernard Salomon: 73 of his motifs seem derived from Salomon and 3 others probably were also, rather than from de Marnef as indicated in the Concordance. For 28 motifs he turned to Zainer or, more probably, to copies of Zainer's series, usually because he had no Salomon model. In 2 instances he drew on Salomon's *Alciati*, and in another he might have done so, but more likely used the same cut in Salomon's *Aesop*. Although the Feyerabend edition in which his woodcuts appeared was printed in 1566, Solis

16. Virgil Solis. *Aesopi Phrygis fabule*. Frankfort: Sigmund Feyerabend, Georg Rab, and Weigand Han, 1566.

died in 1562 and could therefore not have used Plantin's 1565 *Aesop*.

Perhaps Solis persuaded Feyerabend to enlarge the page size of the de Tournes editions he pirated. In any case, because they are larger, Solis's blocks are stronger and clearer than Salomon's, as can be seen in the fairly complicated Jupiter & Frogs (fig. 16). Solis drew the Lyons designs over with some minor adjustments to suit his space and sense of artistic fitness, but he seems not to have bothered to study the text. Yet it is a measure of his enormous ability that the illustrations based on Zainer's motifs are as gracefully Italianate as those that closely imitate Salomon.

Marcus Gheeraerts the Elder of Bruges (1567), London, and Antwerp (1578)

Because Marcus Gheeraerts borrowed motifs from several sources and converted them into fresh Flemish statements, analysis of his 125 *Aesop* illustrations (ca. 94 × 112 mm.)—107 in *De warachtighe fabulen der dieren* (Bruges, 1567) and an additional 18 in *Esbatement moral des animaux* (Antwerp, 1578)—involves some uncertainties (see pls. 4, 10, 18, 27, 35, 47). One would expect Gheeraerts to have been familiar with Plantin's 1565 *Aesop* and to have been stimulated by it to publish his own unique edition, as perhaps he was. Yet he seems not to have used it as a source, partly, no doubt, because it does not contain a number of motifs that Salomon and Solis do provide. And naturally he would prefer the Salomon originals and handsome Solis reproductions to the uninspired van Waesberghen facsimiles of Salomon's designs that Plantin had acquired.

In summary, Virgil Solis (Frankfort, 1566) seems, in spite of the date, to have been Gheeraerts's chief source: 61 motifs (54 in 1567; 7 in 1578). Bernard Salomon (Lyons, 1547, etc.), Solis's main source, seems to have been Gheeraerts's second source: 21 motifs (20 in 1567; 1 in 1578). Gheeraerts preferred to work from the larger Solis woodcuts: in all but 6 instances when he followed Salomon there was no Solis design to follow. A significant 30 of Gheeraerts's motifs (21 in 1567; 9 in 1578) seem either original or from undiscovered sources. Since 25 occur in the Concordance for the first time and 19 for the only time, it seems probable that most of these designs are original. In his dedicatory epistle to Hubert Goltzius, Gheeraerts boasted that some of the fables were his editor de Dene's invention.

The remaining 13 of Gheeraerts's motifs are derived from Zainer, Brant, Janot, combinations of Zainer and Solis and Salomon and Solis, and four emblem books. The indebtedness to Zainer, Brant, and Janot is probably through intermediate editions. Two of Gheeraerts's 1567 motifs seem to come from Plantin's first small *Alciati* series (1565), although they may go back to Plantin's source, Salomon's series (1547, etc.). Of special interest among Gheeraerts's borrowings from emblem books are 2 instances where he seems to have followed the designs of the Mannerist Pierre Eskrich for Rouille's *Alciati*, printed by Bonhomme (Lyons, 1548 , etc.) and also based on Salomon's series. (The Eskrich series is the basis for Plantin's larger *Alciati* series of 1577.) Eskrich's blocks are usually described as woodcuts, but they seem clearly to be burin-engraved in relief on metal, a forerunner of Elisha Kirkall's similar illustrations for Croxall's *Aesop* (1722). Finally, Gheeraerts could have derived his design of an ape using a cat's paw to pull chestnuts out of a fire from part of a Plantin *Sambucus* woodcut, and he seems to have got his phoenix from two vignettes in Plantin's *Paradin*. These attributions are based on propinquity rather than on drawing.

Even more than Salomon and Solis, Gheeraerts made the Aesopic event always seem part of an enveloping scene continuously receding into the distance. Unlike any *Aesop* illustrator before him, he invested the midground with the interest of everday affairs, particularly the river life of his native Low Countries. No matter how extraordinary the main action, it seems credible because life goes tranquilly on

immediately behind it. As we have observed, the choice of
etching as the medium made feasible the introduction of
minute detail, such as tiny figures walking and fishing deep
in the scene. Gheeraerts seems to have been the first artist to
imagine a genuinely particularized environment for the
fables, an expression of the Flemish love of genre. As a
gesture acknowledging the enthusiasm for Italy among his
contemporaries, now and then he turned one of Salomon's
and Solis's mere indications of a castle in the background
into a theatrical Roman ruin. He seems to have ignored the
Flemish verse text of his Bruges friend Edewaerd de Dene
in preparing the plates for *De warachtighe fabulen der
dieren*. It is not clear what his relation was to the French
edition, *Esbatement moral des animaux*, published by
Philippe Galle in Antwerp (1578) with 18 fresh plates by
Gheeraerts. He was working in Antwerp for Galle and
others at the time.

Since animals and birds are the leading characters in the
fables, their treatment is a critical aspect of *Aesop* illustrations. The fifteenth-century woodcuts are merely naive
indicators of the creatures involved. Given the limitations of
small blocks and knife technique, Janot's unknown artist,
Salomon, and Solis produced charming creatures, but they
are necessarily little more than part of the scene. For
Gheeraerts, birds and animals were a major professional
interest, and he based his illustrations and prints on
drawings from life, as far as he was able. Later Antwerp
and Amsterdam publishers issued engravings after his
drawings (including sixteen studies of a bear drawn in
1559) as models for other artists, goldsmiths, and students
to follow. Barlow made drawings for similar instructive
prints in the next century. Gheeraerts's etchings are much
better suited than are woodcuts to suggest the texture of fur
and feathers and the structure of wings, claws, and horns.
Therefore Gheeraert's creatures, including mythological
ones—and, of course, his human beings, especially the
peasants—are so lifelike that they generate their own
separate interest and delight and intensify the believability
of the fables in which they are actors.

5. Chief Seventeenth-Century English Editions

The *Aesop*s of Wenceslaus Hollar and Francis Barlow uniquely dominate seventeenth-century book illustration in England. Francis Cleyn's *Ovid* and *Virgil*, John Baptist Medina's *Paradise Lost*, and a few other illustrated books are worthy of notice. Moreover, Hollar and Barlow illustrated other books. But the burin engravings after drawings by Cleyn and Medina seem academic exercises wholly lacking the vitality, charm, and personal expressiveness of Hollar's and Barlow's etched Aesopic illustrations. Not until Thomas Rowlandson appears will any other English illustrator seem so modern. As noted earlier, it seems coincidental that both Hollar and Barlow had long been accomplished etchers before turning at the same time to illustrate folio editions of *Aesop*, that they both admired the etched fable illustrations of Marcus Gheeraerts the elder, and that their direct predecessor Cleyn, probably in imitation of Gheeraerts, had undertaken to etch his own Aesopic designs instead of having them engraved. Thus, extraordinarily, after tracing through the preceding two hundred years of printing the sources and transmission of the traditional *Aesop* motifs in the seventeenth-century English editions, we arrive at four editions of Aesopic fables, of which three, almost wholly illustrated by two artists, are the chefs d'oeuvre of an entire century.

Francis Cleyn (1651)

Cleyn seems an early example of an artist made uneasy by plagiarism, for he took pains to disguise his borrowings (see pls. 11, 19, 28, 36, 48). Indeed, he was so crafty that when I first compared his illustrations in John Ogilby's *Aesop*

Paraphras'd (1651) with those of Gheeraerts, I was led to
write that despite similarities Cleyn apparently did not use
Gheeraerts as his source. Now it seems clear that he based
at least 46 of his 81 etched designs (ca. 136–48 × 91 mm.)
(on 80 plates) on those in a full collection of Gheeraerts's
plates. Of these 46 designs, 6 are from the 18 Gheeraerts
added in 1578 to the 107 of his 1567 series. In 3 of the 5
instances in which Solis seems to have been Cleyn's model,
Gheeraerts had no illustration, so that Solis seems a logical
source. Cleyn borrowed from 2 designs in the Plantin-
Salomon *Alciati* series and 1 apparently from Zainer,
doubtless by way of a facsimile copy. Of the 27 Cleyn
illustrations listed in the Concordance as original or
borrowed from an unknown source, a few seem to derive
from existing but unidentified sources, but the majority
seem to be original because some of Ogilby's paraphrases
required fresh inventions. In 9 instances no occurrence of
the motif earlier than Cleyn's is recorded, and in 2 others
only an occurrence in *Faerno*. In addition, Cleyn drew a
frontispiece of Aesop, surrounded by animals, addressing a
group of human beings. It seems to be an Ogilby-inspired
advance on the Zainer motif. The plate is signed "F. Clein"
and is evidence for thinking he was both designer and
etcher—he taught Josiah English to etch—and that he did
all the plates in the book.

Cleyn's chief claim to originality is that he read Ogilby's
text and introduced details not in previous designs. In the
first illustration of the Cock & Precious Stone, for example,
he added hens and chicks, a rising sun, a frightened lion,
and a roomful of scholars, all absent from Gheeraerts's
version (see pls. 10, 11). The result here and elsewhere is a
cluttered design, a throwback to the archaic multiple-event
approach Cleyn had used in Sandys's *Ovid* in 1632 and
probably in his tapestries at Mortlake. More interestingly,
Cleyn followed Ogilby now and then in something quite
new, as for instance in the fable of the Ape & Fox, where he
dressed the French ape in a short coat and the Spanish fox
in a long cloak and ruff. But Cleyn had a mechanic's

approach to illustration. As long as his designs were factually correct, he was content. His compositions show no evidence of his considerable experience as a painter and designer. He drew his figures with little sense of their spatial and rhythmic relationships: he placed the main ones large in the foreground with weakly bitten unrelated items here and there in the background. His lack of imaginative projection for the action of the fables and the harshness of his burin-worked etching deny his *Aesop* series the place it might have deserved as the first important one in England since Caxton's and Pynson's and the first English *Aesop* in any degree original.

Wenceslaus Hollar and
"Roderigo" (Dirk) Stoop (1665)

When John Ogilby decided to reprint his 1651 *Aesop Paraphras'd* as a folio, he required a new set of illustrations large enough to face the new type page. His choice of the distinguished draftsman-etcher Wenceslaus (Wenzel, Vá-clav) Hollar to succeed Cleyn promised well, but he spoiled the book by also having Dirk Stoop (1610?–1686?) etch 24 of the 81 plates (ca. 220–50 × 165–95 mm.). Stoop, a native of Utrecht, who had acquired the signature "Roder-igo" in Portugal, completely destroyed the unity of impression of Hollar's 57 plates by the ugliness of his own. Their assignment apparently was to do Cleyn's designs over. Stoop followed Cleyn closely in all but one illustration, where he seems to have included a dog from a Gheeraerts plate. Hollar used Cleyn as his essential purveyor of 44 motifs. He got them on 43 plates because he followed Cleyn's dull device of placing the illustration for the Wolf & Crane in the background of that for the Wolf & Lamb. Hollar turned to Gheeraerts for 9 models, and he combined elements from Gheeraerts and Cleyn 4 times. For the new topical satire of the Dutch that Ogilby added to this second edition as his eighty-second fable, Hollar had to invent his own unique design. The summary of sources for both

Hollar and Stoop is Gheeraerts 9, Cleyn 67, combined 5, and original 1.

Stoop's plates are free enlargements of Cleyn's designs. Conceptually, therefore, they offer traditional illustrations for 24 fables with Cleyn's occasional adjustments, but they make no fresh contribution whatever to the representation of the narratives. Their technical infelicity completes their disqualification from serious consideration. Hereafter Stoop's negative role will be assumed to be understood without further discussion.

Hollar was not by experience, and probably not by inclination, a natural illustrator of belles lettres, but he was a superb draftsman and an etcher of great delicacy and finish, unrivaled for his architectural and topographical prints (see pls. 12, 20, 29, 37, 49). His chief handicap in illustrating Aesop was his lack of firsthand study of animals; only occasionally are his animal actors appealing. He was also overworked and underpaid. In the circumstances it is not remarkable that he depended on the concepts of his predecessors and offered no new interpretations of the fables. Yet he used his talents to create virtually a new art form in England, printed book illustrations as works of independent charm.

As noted earlier, Gheeraerts had brought etching to England a century before in his twenty plates for Jan van der Noot's Théâtre (John Day, 1568). He had introduced to English book illustration realistic detail, textural effects, and tonal subtleties unknown to woodcuts. In Edward Benlowes's Theophila (1652) Francis Barlow had demonstrated how magnificently well-conceived and well-executed etchings could illustrate a difficult poetic text. Hollar felt constrained to take his motifs mainly from Cleyn, but he got the inspiration for his treatment from Gheeraerts's wholly integrated scene where the actors can, if they wish, walk on visible ground from where they stand gradually back to the horizon. Without having the kind of imagination—or, probably, the time—to paraphrase Aesopic designs as Ogilby had done the fables, Hollar devoted his

17. Wenceslaus Hollar. John Ogilby, *The Fables of Aesop, Para-phras'd in Verse.* London: Thomas Roycroft for J. Ogilby, 1665.

efforts to recreating other men's foreground action in fastidious detail as, for instance, he did Cleyn's Ape & Fox in his version (fig. 17). He reestablished the animal and human characters in a fully articulated larger scene, imitating Gheeraerts in faithfully rendered costumes, interiors, rustic cottages, and stately castles and surpassing him in the decorative backdrops of ancient trees, majestic mountains, and spacious harbors.

Hollar's personal touch is in his extensive and delicate shading, subtly distributed in areas of contrasting dark and light in the foreground and moving smoothly to the lightly bitten background so that his etchings often take on a lithographic richness. On these large plates Hollar achieved a sense of great openness, of airy interiors and plein-air landscapes, but the action often seems subordinate to the scene. Thus, though some of Hollar's plates are among the most striking and delightful in any English book, in his *Aesop* series charm of effect transcends expressiveness of interpretation. It must also be admitted that a number suffer from too much dark cross-hatching.

Francis Barlow (1666)

The most surprising fact about Francis Barlow's use of traditional motifs for the 110 illustrations (ca. 128 × 158 mm.) of his French-English-Latin *Aesop's Fables* (1666) is the extent of his sources. Even after making allowances for doubtful and erroneous attributions, it seems that Barlow drew on all of the chief sources except Pfister. It is likely that he followed late editions or copies of Zainer, Janot, and Salomon, and like Cleyn he could have followed Gheeraerts's designs in the 1578, 1579, or later editions. Yet Barlow seems to have based only about half of his 110 designs on those of Gheeraerts—46 plus 7 in which a Gheeraerts motif is one of the components in combined sources and 3 in which it may be the source in unassigned instances. Barlow probably turned to Cleyn for a surprising 13 motifs and 5 others in borrowings from more than one source. From Solis he took 8 motifs and parts of 3 others, mainly because Gheeraerts did not illustrate those fables. His remaining apparent borrowings were from Zainer 2, Salomon 3 and 1 with Cleyn, Plantin 1, and Janot 1 with Gheeraerts. Then 25 designs seem original or less likely, gathered from sources unknown. Only 5 of these 25 illustrate fables not listed as illustrated by others.

As already noted, Barlow had shown that he was a draftsman of great ability and an interpretive illustrator of originality and power in the ten plates he etched for Edward Benlowes's difficult book-length religious poem *Theophila* (1652). He faced nothing so formidable in *Aesop*, but he elected, in a spirit perhaps of respectful competition with Gheeraerts, in the main to follow traditional concepts, much as a composer develops themes from folk songs (see pls. 5, 13, 21, 30, 38, 42, 50). Gheeraerts influenced him profoundly in two ways: in placing his main actors solidly within a realistic contemporary environment and in drawing his birds and animals with loving care but without humorous condescension or anthropomorphic characteristics. Gheeraerts had been one of the earliest European artists to make a specialty of animals; Barlow was the first modern Englishman to do so, and he has had few equals. He loved all wild and domestic creatures, and he used the *Aesop* to celebrate their grace and dignity, as in his Leopard & Fox (fig. 18). Wherever he could, he placed them where most of them belonged, among the familiar English farms and fields that he also loved. Yet—and the point is important—Barlow followed Gheeraerts, and perhaps outdid him, in turning fable illustrations from humorous pantomime or stylized morality plays into often moving domestic drama, and he achieved a sense of credibility that is the mark of distinguished illustration. His treatment of the traditional motif for the farfetched fable of the stag that hid from pursuit in an ox stall is an example of this credibility (fig. 19).

Fortunately, Barlow himself etched all of the plates for his 110 fables. He also etched an oval animal border for an

18. Francis Barlow. *Aesop's Fables.* London: William Godbid for F.
Barlow, 1666.

engraved title page and a frontispiece of Aesop among the
friendly animals. True, he told John Evelyn that he was no
etcher, and he turned over most of his designs for the 1687
Life of Aesop plates to Thomas Dudley to etch. He etched
as Gheeraerts did, as a means of reproducing drawings,
with strong linear effects and without the subtle tonal
values of Hollar's plates. It is also true that he sometimes
overdid the use of a burin to reinforce the outlines of main
characters. Several of his plates seem less finished than the
rest, as though made from early drafts. Yet only Barlow's
own etching does full justice to the beauty of his drawings of
animals and birds, their pelts and plumage and attitudes,
and to background details such as a hunt flying across an
airy field. With Gheeraerts, Rembrandt, Hollar, Rowlandson, George Cruikshank, Hablot K. Browne, William

19. Francis Barlow. *Aesop's Fables*. London: William Godbid for F. Barlow, 1666.

Strang, Edmund Blampied, and Dunoyer de Segonzac, Barlow demonstrated that etching can be a perfect medium for illustrating books

Ogilby's Aesopics *(1668)*

To recoup his losses on the 1665 edition of *Aesop Paraphras'd* in the Great Fire of 1666, John Ogilby not only brought out another edition in 1668 but boldly added fifty more fables under the title *Aesopics*, together with two other verse narratives, *Androcleus*, illustrated by Barlow, and *The Ephesian Matron*, illustrated by Hollar. Because some of the new fables in *Aesopics* have the same characters, only forty-one of the fifty are illustrated. Since 3 of Hollar's 1665 plates are used again and in two other instances 1 plate illustrates two fables, there are 36 new illustrations in *Aesopics*. Hollar etched 19 illustrations on 18 plates, and it appears that Barlow drew the designs for 18 on 17 plates. Josiah English, a pupil of Cleyn, etched 1 in a poor imitation of Hollar.

The sources of Hollar's 19 *Aesopics* motifs are Solis 1, Gheeraerts 2, Barlow 4, Stoop 1, Hollar 1, and original 10. Borrowing 6 motifs from Ogilby's and Barlow's recent editions, reusing 3 of his own *Aesop Paraphras'd* plates, and calling on Barlow to share the job suggest that Hollar was under some unusual pressure when he worked on the *Aesopics*.

Barlow did not etch his plates. Richard Gaywood etched 8, signing 1 and dating it 1668. Of the remaining 10 illustrations, one anonymous hand engraved 7 on 6 plates and another etched 3. Barlow's sources for motifs are Zainer 3, Solis 2, Gheeraerts 2, Barlow 2, Solis and Barlow 1, and original 8. Josiah English used a Barlow 1666 design for his model.

Consolidated, the sources for the 38 *Aesopics* motifs are the following: Zainer 3, Solis 3, Gheeraerts 4, Hollar 1, Stoop 1, Barlow 7, Solis and Barlow 1, and original 18. As a whole the volume is too mixed in effects and quality of execution to be the equal of either Hollar's 1665 *Aesop Paraphras'd* or Barlow's 1666 *Aesop's Fables*. Individually, however, a few of Hollar's plates are among the most impressive of English illustrations.

Barlow's Life of Aesop (1687)

The thrice-told Life of Aesop by Planudes in the front of Barlow's polyglot 1666 edition takes up eighty-eight unadorned pages. To correct this defect, in the 1687 edition Barlow added one of the most elaborate Life series ever published, 31 numbered plates inserted as a unit between the English account and the French. They are full folio-page size illustrations with a cartouche at the bottom of each plate for engraved text. To find Barlow's source, we do not have to make the same number of comparisons as for the fable illustrations. Pfister, Janot, Gheeraerts, and Ogilby had not printed the Life, and Salomon had not illustrated the one in the de Tournes editions. Solis had derived his Life cuts from Zainer's, though like Caxton doubtless from copies.

Enough of Barlow's Life of Aesop designs vary from the Zainer concepts to indicate a variant source. It seems to be Pieter van der Borcht's small etched and engraved series (37 × 53 mm.) in *Les fables et la vie d'Esope* (Jan Mourentorf, Antwerp, 1593). Van der Borcht seems to have made facsimile copies of the woodcut series in Jerome de Marnef's Paris *Aesopi Phrygis et aliorum fabulae*. The 1582 edition was de Marnef's first with the Life illustrated (I have seen only the 1585 reprint). Or van der Borcht could have followed the hypothetical source of de Marnef's set. Barlow followed van der Borcht when he varied slightly from de Marnef, though Barlow's borrowing was always completely free and original. In the system used here in the Concordance, each design would be assigned the symbol (=), indicating enough similarity to make borrowing probable, not absolutely certain. But since van der Borcht omits the exposure of Xanthus's wife, Barlow must either have based his design for that illustration on de Marnef's or conceivably have based all of his designs on a series unknown to me though closely linked to van der Borcht's series.

Barlow contributed at least two fresh qualities to the Life of Aesop series. He bestowed dignity on Aesop, sometimes treated as a comic figure by earlier artists, and he gave fashionable baroque characteristics to the costumes and settings, as in one of Aesop's displays of wit before royalty (fig. 20). But the transmission of the Life designs is so separate from that of the fable illustrations that no further account seems called for. It is worth noting that in 1704, the year of Barlow's death, Etienne Roger brought out *Les fables d'Esope* in Amsterdam *avec les figures dessinées & gravées par F. Barlouw, d'une manière savante & pittores-*

Of all the graces, Heaven in man designd,
None charmes us like the beautyes of the mind,
The fickle forme, each accident destroys,
But witt deverts with new and lasting joys.

2J

20.   Francis Barlow. *Aesop's Fables*. Second edition. London: Henry
Hills, Jr., for F. Barlow, 1687.

que. He used almost all of Barlow's 1666 and 1687 plates, including the original frontispiece, with a French translation of Sir Roger L'Estrange's famous English translation (1692, 1699). In 1799 La Fontaine's *Recueil des fables d'Esop et autres mythologistes* appeared in Paris with faithful copies of Barlow's plates by Augustin Legrand. And the polyglot *Hundert Fabeln nach Aesop und den grössten Fabelndichtern aller Zeiten* published in Berlin in 1830 contains a frontispiece and 100 colored engravings based on Barlow's illustrations. Thus the story of Aesop in England as manifested in seventeenth-century book illustration closes without ending.

Concordance

6. Bibliography of *Aesop* Editions

Note: The numbers of illustrations given here do not include portraits, decorative designs, or other incidental cuts or repeats unless specifically noted.

Continental Sources

1461 Albrecht Pfister, Bamberg. Ulrich Boner, *Der Edelstein*. German. Fol. 103 woodcut fable illustrations (ca. 77 × 105 mm.) by an unknown artist. Not at BL.[1] My references are to the photographic facsimile reprint of the unique Berlin copy of the undated edition plus six pages from the unique Wolfenbüttel copy of the 14 February 1461 edition, with an introduction by Paul O. Kristeller. Graphische Gesellschaft 1. Ausserordentliche Veröffentlichung. Berlin: B. Cassirer, 1908. BL: K.T.C.121.b.9. Kristeller finds no evidence to support the belief that the Wolfenbüttel edition precedes the Berlin. Since the point is of no importance here, I use the date 1461.

[ca. **1476**] Johann Zainer, Ulm. *Vita Esopi et Fabulae*. Heinrich Steinhöwel, tr. Latin and German. Fol. According to Weil, frontispiece and 192 woodcut illustrations by an unknown artist. No copy at BL. My references are to Anton Sorg's Latin edition (Augsburg, [1480?]), *Vita Esopi et fabulae* with the original woodcuts (ca. 77 × 105 mm.): 1

---

1. In 1972 the library and library staff in the British Museum came under the administration of the British Library (BL). The Department of Prints and Drawings remains a part of the British Museum (BM: P&D).

frontispiece, 28 Life illustrations, plus 1 repeat, 1 author-presentation cut, and 163 fable illustrations. BL: G.7805.

1501   Jacob [Wolff] of Pfortzheim, Basel. *Esope appologi siue mythologia cum quibusdam carminus et fabularum additionibus Sebastiani Brant.* Latin. 8°. Part I: Facsimile copies of Zainer's series, most reversed, with 3 new woodcuts. Part II: 138(?) woodcut fable illustrations (ca. 77 X 117 mm.) plus 2 repeats. Probably by the "Master of the Grüninger office," according to Christian L. Küster. BL: G.7809 and 86.k.1. Neither BL copy has sig. i7 and i8. Perhaps this explains Küster's count of 143 blocks in Part II. The edition is referred to here as Sebastian Brant's.

1542   Denys Janot, Paris. *Les fables du tresancien Esope Phrygien.* G. Corrozet, tr. French. 8°. 100 woodcut fable illustrations by an unidentified Italianate hand. No copy at BL. References are to the Bodleian copy of Janot's 1544 reprint with the same 100 woodcuts (ca. 31 X 51 mm.). Bodl: Mason FF 221.

1547   Jean de Tournes and Guillaume Gazeau, Lyons. *Les fables d'Esope Phrygien.* G. Corrozet, tr., A. du Moulin, ed. French. 16°. According to Ruth Mortimer, 99 woodcut fable illustrations, plus 1 repeat, by Bernard Salomon. No copy at BL. References are to de Tournes's editions of 1551, 16°, with 41 woodcut illustrations (ca. 36 X 46 mm.) (V&A: 88.D.18); 1564, 16°, said to be a reprint of the 1556 edition, with 91 illustrations (V&A: 88.D.39); and 1570, 16°, with 61 illustrations (BL: G.7712), including 29 not in the 1564 edition. Also used: Jerome de Marnef's *Aesopi Phrygis et aliorum fabulae* (Paris, 1561), 16°, with ca. 115 woodcut illustrations (ca. 36 X 46 mm.), which include facsimile copies of Salomon's series (BL: 57.k.23), and de Marnef and D. Girault Cavellat's edition (Paris, 1585), 16°, which includes woodcut illustrations (ca. 36 X 49 mm.) of Aesop's life (BL: 1067.b.14). See p. 77 for explanation of bracketed Salomon entries out of chronological order. As a matter of expediency, four of

Salomon's designs are represented in the Plates here by de Marnef's facsimile copies.

1563 Vincenzio Luchino, Rome. Gabriello Faerno, *Fabulae centum*. Latin. 8°. 100 etched and engraved illustrations (ca. 145 × 107 mm.), now attributed to Pirro Ligorio. BL: G.9709. Christopher Plantin (Antwerp, 1567) brought out a 16° Latin edition with 100 woodcut illustrations. They are faithful reduced copies of the 1563 plates. They were drawn by Pieter van der Borcht and cut by Arnold Nicolai and Gerard van Kampen. These blocks were used in several later editions, even as late as Francis Foppen's (Brussels, 1682), which is the earliest one containing them at the British Library. BL: 637.b.17. The 1563 edition is noted in the Concordance only when it contains the first occurrence of a motif recorded here. The Plantin edition is not entered because neither it nor the Rome edition seems the source for the few similar designs in the Concordance.

1565 Christopher Plantin, Antwerp. *Aesopi Phrygis, et aliorum fabulae*. Latin. 12°. 76 woodcut fable illustrations (ca. 35 × 47 mm.), facsimile copies of Salomon's designs except for 6 blocks from Plantin's emblem books. Plantin got the 70 blocks from the Antwerp printer Jan van Waesberghen. See p. 46. Not at BL or V&A. Xerographs of the copy at the Bibliothèque royale Albert Ier (VB.6828^2.A.L.P.) were used for reference.

1566 Sigmund Feyerabend, Georg Rab, and Weigand Han, Frankfort. *Aesopi Phrygis fabule*. Latin. 8°. 13 woodcut illustrations for Aesop's life signed with the monogram of Virgil Solis and 190 illustrations (ca. 48 × 67 mm.) for the fables (including numerous repeats that do not fit their fables). 119 are signed with Solis's monogram, 1 is signed HH, and the rest are unsigned. BL: 12305.aaa.41.

1567, 26 August Pieter de Clerck for Marcus Gheeraerts, Bruges. Edewaerd de Dene, *De warachtighe Fabulen der dieren*. Flemish. 8°. 107 etched fable illustrations (ca. 94 ×

112 mm.) by Marcus Gheeraerts the elder. BM (P&D):
157.b.18.

1578   Gerard Smits for Philippe Galle, Antwerp. [Pieter
Heyns(?) and E.VV.], *Esbatement moral des animaux.*
French. 8°. 125 etched fable illustrations, the original 107
from the 1567 edition plus 18 new designs (ca. 94 × 112
mm.) by Marcus Gheeraerts the elder. BL: C.125.d.23. In
1579 Galle published Arnold Freitag's Latin version,
Mythologia ethica, printed by Christopher Plantin. It
contains in the same order the same 125 plates as the
French edition. BL: 12305.dd.19. They reappear in later
books such as Joost van Vondel's *Vörstelijcke warande der
dieren* (Amsterdam, 1617).

Emblem Book Sources

1531, 14 February.   Heinrich Steyner, Augsburg. Andrea
Alciati, *Emblematum liber.* Latin. 8°. 98 woodcuts (36 ×
60 mm.; a few 60 × 36 mm.), said to be by Hans
Schäuffelein or Jörg Breu the elder. BL: C.57.a.11. Refer-
ences are to corrected second edition, 6 April 1531. BL:
C.175.i.13.

1534   Chrestien Wechel, Paris. Andrea Alciati, *Emblematum libellus.* Latin. 8°. 111 woodcuts (66 × 62 mm.; a few
larger) said to be by Jean Jollat after an unknown artist.
BL: 683.d.29(3).

1547   Jean de Tournes and Guillaume Gazeau, Lyons.
Andrea Alciati, *Emblematum liber.* Latin. 16°. 113 wood-
cuts (37 × 51 mm.) by Bernard Salomon. BL:
C.125.cc.19.

1548   Macé Bonhomme for Guillaume Rouille (Rouillé,
Roville), Lyons. Andrea Alciati, *Emblemes.* French. 8°.
150 metal relief blocks (60 × 63 mm.), burin-engraved by
Pierre Eskrich (Cruche, Vase), and 14 trees (68 × 42
mm.). Not at BL. References are to the 1549 edition. BL:
C.62.b.20.

1557 Jean de Tournes and Guillaume Gazeau, Lyons. Claude Paradin, *Devises Héroïques*. French. 8°. De Tournes's 1551 edition enlarged to 182 woodcut vignettes of assorted sizes (rough average ca. 55 mm. high) by Bernard Salomon (?). BL: C.31.b.33.

1562 Christopher Plantin, Antwerp. Claude Paradin, *Heroica [Les devises héroïques]*. Latin. 16°. 215 woodcut vignettes (rough average ca. 55 mm. high) cut by Arnold Nicolai and Gerard van Kampen (?), mainly facsimile copies of the 1557 Lyons edition designs. BL: 607.a.23.

1564 Christopher Plantin, Antwerp. Ioannis Sambucus, *Emblemata*. Latin. 8°. 166 woodcut devices (48 × 56 mm.) and 46 medals designed by Pieter van der Borcht, Pieter Huys, and Lucas d'Heere and cut by Arnold Nicolai, Gerard van Kampen, and Cornelius Muller. BL: 90.i.28.

1565 Christopher Plantin, Antwerp. Andrea Alciati, *Emblematum clarissimi, viri, D. Andreae Alciati libri II*. Latin. 16°. 111 woodcuts (ca. 35 × 47 mm.), facsimile copies of Salomon's designs by Geoffroy Ballain cut by Arnold Nicolai and Gerard van Kampen. BL (MSS): Add MSS 17488. The Museum Plantin-Moretus copy is said to have 112 cuts. 24 blocks were added in the 20 October 1566 edition. Not in BL. Ballain of Paris was paid a little more for drawing the designs on the blocks than the cutters were for cutting them. Another edition dated 1567 (V&A: RC.D.31.) in fact came out before 8 September 1566. The 1566 edition, printed between 8 September and 20 October, contains two fewer cuts. The above information was generously given by Dr. L. Voet, Director of the Museum Plantin-Moretus in Antwerp, where the original blocks still are. I have depended for comparisons on the 1573 Plantin edition (BL: 012305.de.10), which includes the 1565 and 1566 cuts.

English Editions

1651 Thomas Warren for Andrew Crook. John Ogilby, *The Fables of Aesop, Paraphras'd in Verse*. 4°. 81 etched fable illustrations on 80 plates (ca. 142 × 92 mm.) (nos. 14 and 15 on one plate) by Francis Cleyn. BL: C.77.c.12.

1665 Thomas Roycroft for the author. John Ogilby, *The Fables of Aesop, Paraphras'd in Verse.* Second edition. Fol. 82 etched fable illustrations on 81 plates (ca. 222 × 165 mm.) (nos. 14 and 15 on one plate and an illustration for new fable 82 added) by Wenceslaus Hollar and "Roderigo" (Dirk) Stoop. BL: 1872.a.12(1).

1666 William Godbid for Francis Barlow. *Aesop's Fables in English, French & Latin. The English* [fables in verse] *by Tho. Philipott, Esq; The French and Latin by Rob. Codrington, M.A.* Fol. 110 etched fable illustrations (ca. 225 × 160 mm.) by Francis Barlow with the fable in English engraved beneath each illustration. BL: C.70.h.3.

1668 Thomas Roycroft for the author. John Ogilby, *Aesopic's: Or a second Collection of Fables, Paraphras'd in Verse.* Fol. 36 new etched and burin-engraved fable illustrations (ca. 250 × 190 mm.), plus 3 from the 1665 edition, by Wenceslaus Hollar, Josiah English, and Francis Barlow. BL: 1872.a.12(2).

1687 H. Hills jun. for Francis Barlow. *Aesop's Fables with His Life . . . Newly Translated* [i.e., the English verse redone by Aphra Behn]. Fol. 31 new etched illustrations for Aesop's life (ca. 240 × 160 mm.) designed by Barlow and etched by Barlow and Thomas Dudley, together with the 110 fable illustrations from the 1666 edition. BL: G.7848, 671.1.6, and C.132.i.63 (from Chatsworth; with binding of the duke of Devonshire, to whom this edition is dedicated).

7. Charts of Main Sources and Lines of Transmission

See text for individual variations.

(a) *Aesopic Fables*

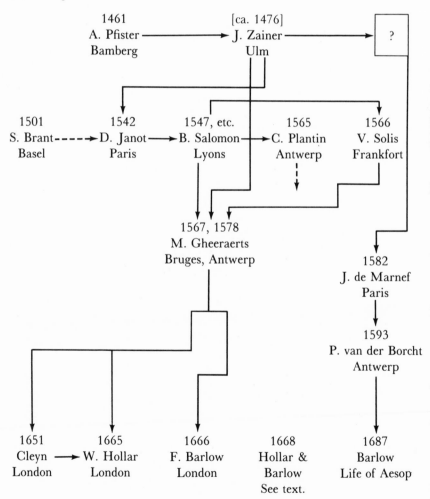

1461
A. Pfister ⟶ J. Zainer ⟶ ?
Bamberg   Ulm
[ca. 1476]

1501   1542   1547, etc.   1565   1566
S. Brant----▶D. Janot⟶B. Salomon⟶C. Plantin   V. Solis
Basel   Paris   Lyons   Antwerp   Frankfort

1567, 1578
M. Gheeraerts
Bruges, Antwerp

1582
J. de Marnef
Paris

1593
P. van der Borcht
Antwerp

1651   1665   1666   1668   1687
Cleyn ⟶ W. Hollar   F. Barlow   Hollar &   Barlow
London   London   London   Barlow   Life of Aesop
                                            See text.

(b) *Emblem Books*

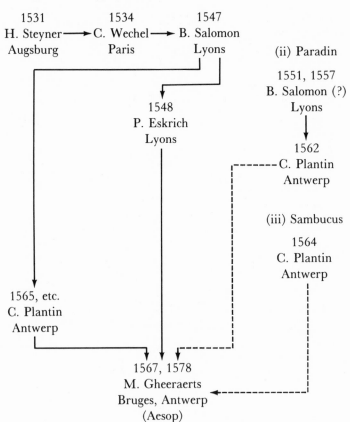

(i) Alciati

1531	1534	1547
H. Steyner ⟶	C. Wechel ⟶	B. Salomon
Augsburg	Paris	Lyons

(ii) Paradin

1551, 1557
B. Salomon (?)
Lyons

1548
P. Eskrich
Lyons

1562
C. Plantin
Antwerp

(iii) Sambucus

1564
C. Plantin
Antwerp

1565, etc.
C. Plantin
Antwerp

1567, 1578
M. Gheeraerts
Bruges, Antwerp
(Aesop)

8. Explanation of Style and Symbols of Indebtedness

For the purpose of visual identification of illustrations, the titles of the fables in the following list are made up of the generic names of the chief actors, not necessarily of the names commonly used in English editions. Titles often occur in reverse order in different editions. To avoid endless cross-references, it is assumed that a reader not finding an entry for Fly & Ant will look under Ant & Fly. Usually the most easily identifiable element comes first, as in Bear & Travelers, but designs with similar elements, as those with a birdcatcher, are grouped together. I have tried to choose the most usual term of identification; e.g., *snake,* not *adder* or *serpent.* Fabulists freely vary the names, the kinds, and the numbers of characters, and some characters, especially birds, are hard to identify in small designs. I have tried to warn against special hazards, but many go unnoted. In individual editions the reader must expect variations from the brief description of the design given here beneath each title.

The editions noted are those described in detail in the preceding pages. The fable books are indicated here only by the initials of the first two printers—Albrecht Pfister (AP) and Johann Zainer (JZ)—then by those of the author Sebastian Brant (SB^1 and SB^2 for parts 1 and 2) and the printer Denys Janot (DJ), and thereafter by those of the artist Bernard Salomon (BS), the printers Jerome de Marnef (JdeM) and Christopher Plantin (CP), and the artists Virgil Solis (VS), Marcus Gheeraerts (MG), Francis Cleyn (FC), Wenceslaus Hollar (WH), "Roderigo" Stoop (RS), and Francis Barlow (FB). The names of printers and authors of emblem books are spelled out. The inclusion of the 1501 Brant *Aesop* and the 1563 *Faerno* is explained on p. 40 and p. 69 respectively. Brackets are used around the initials of artists in assigning unsigned blocks where the identity of the artists may be in doubt.

The following symbols indicate what seems the approximate degree of indebtedness:

(*)   Either an original design or a borrowing of indeterminate originality from a source not noted. In English editions the design is much more likely to be original than in earlier continental editions.

(=)   Similarity of action and relations among the foreground characters or other elements makes the borrowing from the indicated source or one closely related seem probable. Occasionally more than one source seems to have been consulted.

(≐)   Close similarity of the main elements or of some special detail makes borrowing from the indicated source seem certain.

(+)   Some significant change (not necessarily an addition) in a design still recognizably borrowed, probably from the source noted.

(?)   Source uncertain but probably one of those noted. A question mark after initials (FC?) suggests that, while the relationship indicated seems probable, it lacks strong similarities or is unusual enough to be open to question.

This is hardly a scientific system of classification, the distinction between (=) and (+) being the most liable to waver. But the main purpose of the table is to help the user to make his own comparisons and judgments.

Space does not permit comparison of backgrounds, except in unusually revealing instances, as in Hollar's plate for the Lion & Mouse. Backgrounds often do provide clues or reinforcing evidence of relationship, but in general they vary much more than the basic composition in ways that are meaningless for our purpose.

As I have already noted, my references to Zainer's blocks are based on Anton Sorg's (1480?) edition. Wherever a later woodcut seems derived from one of Zainer's designs and I so indicate, it has to be understood that the copyist may have been looking at any of several editions, like Sorg's, that use the original blocks or at one of the numerous copies, such as Gerard Leeu's facsimile set or Caxton's awkward but faithful copies of copies. In terms of essential conception and treatment, the designs are still those of Zainer's hand, the anonymous person who drew them and may have cut them too. It is conceivable that some of the later artists took their suggestions from Pfister's *Edelstein* rather than from any version of the Zainer designs, but I have seen very limited evidence of such borrowing. The same sort of equivalence that applies to Zainer's editions and copies of them also applies to Janot's, Salomon's, and Gheeraerts's editions and close copies of them.

The bracketed editions of Salomon's *Aesop* are listed out of their chronological order to indicate the probability that the source is not the later available de Tournes editions but the 1547 first edition or another early edition, for which no copy was available to me. The probability seems a certainty when the 1544 Janot, 1561 de Marnef, or 1565 Plantin edition is also present.

References are to signatures, pages, plates, or fables, whichever is most conspicuous in a particular edition.

9. Concordance of the Sources of Motifs Used in Seventeenth-Century English *Aesop* Illustrations

Note: Alphabetizing is initially by the first main noun and then letter by letter: thus, Sick Lion, Lion & Goat, Doctor Lion & Horse. See pp. 75–77 for explanation of terms, abbreviations, etc. Location is given by signature, page, fable, or plate in specific books.

Adder. See Snake.

1. *Angler & Little Fish*
   An angler holding a little fish.

[1480?] JZ oij^r (*)
1571 BS p. 178 (+JZ)
1666 FB p. 157 (+BS)

2. *Ant & Fly*
   Ants at foot of a tree; a fly on the ground or in the air.

1461	AP p. 49	(*)	1566	VS fab. 89	(≐BS)
[1480?]	JZ f8^v	(+AP)	1567	MG p. 110	(≐VS)
1544	DJ E5^v	(+JZ)	1651	FC pl. 33	(=MG)
1564	BS p. 154	(≐DJ)	1665	WH pl. 33	(≐MG)
1565	CP p. 188	(≐BS)	1666	FB p. 97	(=?)

3. *Ant & Grasshopper*
   Ant(s) at foot of a tree; a grasshopper.

1461	AP p. 51	(*)	1567	MG p. 26	(≐VS)
[1480?]	JZ i8^r	(+AP)	1666	FB p. 99	(=MG)
1544	DJ Oii^v	(=JZ)	1668	WH opp. p. 27	(=MG)
1551	BS p. 263	(≐DJ)			
1566	VS fab. 108	(≐BS)			

4. *Ape & Cat's Paw*
An ape holding a cat's paw before a fire.

1564 C. Plantin, *Sambucus*   1567 MG p. 210 (+CP
      p. 110 (*)   1564?)

5. *Ape & Fox*
An ape and a fox facing one another.

[1480?] JZ h6^v (*)	1567 MG p. 74 (≐VS)
1544 DJ F8^v (=JZ)	1651 FC pl. 34 (*)
1551 BS p. 155 (=DJ)	1665 WH pl. 34 (≐FC)
1565 CP p. 221 (≐BS)	1666 FB p. 57 (+MG)
1566 VS fab. 29 (≐BS)	

6. *Ape & Young*
An ape holding a baby ape; a young one nearby.

1501 SB^2 Ii^v (*) See p.	1544 DJ Oi^v (+DJ
40.	[1539?])
[1539?] DJ *Le théâtre des*	1564 BS p. 218 (=DJ)
bons engins Giiii^v	1566 VS fab.186 (≐BS)
(=SB^2)	1567 MG p. 172 (+VS)

7. *Apes Dancing*
Apes, dancing for a human audience, distracted by nuts.

1567 MG p. 62 (*)	1651 FC pl. 55 (*)
[Perry, p. 517]†	1665 RS pl. 55 (≐FC)

8. *Ass & Boar (Lion)*
An ass facing a boar or lion. See p. 38.

1461 AP p. 19 (*)	1566 VS fab. 66 (≐JZ)
[1480?] JZ d8^r (≐AP)	VS fab. 115 (≐BS)
1501 SB^1 d6^v (*)	1567 MG p. 40 (=VS)
1544 DJ B7^v (=SB^1)	1651 FC pl. 11 (=MG)
[1571 BS p. 229 (=DJ)]‡	1665 WH pl. 11 (=FC)
1565 CP p. 173 (≐BS)	1666 FB p. 205 (≐FC)

†See p. 45 for references to Perry.

‡See p. 77 for explanation of bracketed Salomon entries out of chronological order.

9. *Envious Ass & Horses*
An ass frightened by a cavalry battle.

1563   V. Luchino, *Faerno*   1665   [RS] pl. 69   ($\doteq$FC)
       pl. 84   (*)
1651   FC pl. 69   (*)   [Per-
       ry, p. 486]

10. *Ass & Thistle*
An ass, its panier bulging with food, eating a thistle.
See pls. 1–5.

1531   H. Steyner, *Alciati*   1565   C. Plantin, *Alciati* p.
       C6^r (*)   93   ($\doteq$BS 1547)
1534   C. Wechel, *Alciati* p.   1567   MG p. 174   (=BS
       55   (+HS 1531)   *Alciati*)
1547   BS, *Alciati* p. 53   1666   FB p. 11   ($\doteq$MG)
       (=CW 1534)

11. *Ass, Bullock, Mule, & Camel*
An ass, bullock, and mule facing a camel.

1567   MG p. 106   (*)

12. *Ass in Lion's Skin*
An ass covered by a lion's skin led, or beaten, by a man
with a club.

1461   AP p. 100   (*)   1651   FC pl. 70   ($\doteq$VS)
[1480?]   JZ niiij^r (+AP)   1665   RS pl. 70   ($\doteq$FC)
1566   VS fab. 45   ($\doteq$JZ)   1666   FB p. 145   (+FC?)

13. *Ass, Master, & Jupiter*
A tanner beating an ass carrying hides; (above) Jupiter.

1544   DJ I8^v (*)   1567   MG p. 206   (=VS)
1564   BS p. 194   ($\doteq$DJ)   1651   FC pl. 68   (+MG)
1566   VS fab. 112   ($\doteq$BS)   1665   RS pl. 68   (=FC)

14. *Ass, Master, & Little Dog*
One or two servants beating an ass rearing before a
seated man holding a lap dog.

1461   AP p. 25   (*)   [1480?]   JZ eiiij^r (=AP)

1544	DJ Ciiii^v (=JZ)	1651	FC pl. 24 (=MG)
1564	BS p. 136 (≐DJ)	1665	WH pl. 24 (=MG,
1565	CP p. 180 (≐BS)		FC)
1566	VS fab. 160 (≐BS)	1666	FB p. 163 (=MG?)
1567	MG p. 126 (=VS)		

15. Basilisk & Weasel

A large cocklike fowl with a rodent's tail pursued by a weasel wearing a garland.

1567 MG p. 4 (*)

16. Bear & Beehives

A bear tormented by bees from upset beehives.

1567	MG p. 146 (*)	1665	WH pl. 44 (+FC)
1651	FC pl. 44 (≐MG)	1666	FB p. 173 (=FC?)

17. Bear & Two Travelers

A bear (wolf) sniffing a prostrate man; a man in a tree.

1461	AP p. 109 (*)	1567	MG p. 112 (≐BS)
[1480?]	JZ n6^r (+AP)	1651	FC pl. 52 (≐MG)
1544	DJ Miiii^v (+JZ?)	1665	WH pl. 52 (=MG,
1564	BS p. 62 (=DJ)		FC)
1565	CP p. 207 (≐BS)	1666	FB p. 175 (≐MG)

18. Hunted Beaver

A beaver biting himself as a hunter and dogs close in.

1501	SB^2 Liij^r (*)	1565	C. Plantin, Alciati p.
1531	H. Steyner, Alciati E3^r (*)		154 (≐BS 1547) Single border
1534	C. Wechel, Alciati p. 90 (=HS 1531)	1565	CP, Aesop p. 88 (≐BS) Double border
1547	BS, Alciati p. 88 (+CW 1534) Single border	1566	VS fab. 33 (≐BS)
		1666	FB p. 39 (=VS?)
1551	BS, Aesop p. 160 (BS 1547 Alciati block)		

19. Belly & Members

A naked male body lying on the ground; or, a Humpty-Dumpty figure.

1461	AP p. 90	(*)	1651	FC pl. 47 (*)
[1480?]	JZ h6ʳ	(+AP)	1665	WH pl. 47 (≐FC)
1544	DJ F7ᵛ	(≐JZ)	1666	FB p. 109 (≐BS)
1564	BS p. 164	(≐DJ)		

20. Birdcatcher & Bird (I)

See also *Snake & Birdcatcher; Birdcatcher, Ant, & Dove.*

A man kneeling beside a net holding a bird by the neck with one hand.

1544	DJ Niiiiᵛ	(*)	1566	VS fab. 55 (≐BS)
1551	BS p. 185	(≐DJ)	1567	MG p. 108 (≐VS)
1565	CP p. 162	(≐BS)	1666	FB p. 137 (≐MG)

21. Birdcatcher & Birds (II)

See also *Birdcatcher, Storks, & Geese.*

A man working a net snare; birds on the ground or in the air.

1501	SB² Lijᵛ	(*)	1566	VS fab. 46 (≐BS)
1544	DJ Iz[K]5ᵛ	(=SB²?)	1567	MG p. 30 (+VS)
1551	BS p. 176	(≐DJ)		

22. Birdcatcher & Birds (III)

A man beside bird traps holding a bird in both hands; a hooded falcon.

1666   FB p. 181   (*)

23. Birdcatcher, Ant, & Dove

A kneeling man with a bird net being bitten on the foot by an ant; a dove in a tree.

[1480?]	JZ m7ʳ	(*)	1565	CP p. 94 (≐BS)
1544	DJ I5ᵛ	(=JZ)	1566	VS fab. 175 (≐JZ)
1551	BS p. 169	(≐DJ)	1666	FB p. 217 (=BS)

24. *Birdcatcher, Cuckoo, & Kite*

A man looking at a large bird under a net; smaller birds feeding.

1567   MG p. 130   (*)

25. *Birdcatcher, Storks, & Geese (Crane)*

See also *Birdcatcher & Birds (II); Geese & Cranes.*

A man holding a net with birds inside; long-necked birds running or flying away.

[1480?]	JZ m6^r (*)	1567	MG p. 116 (=BS)
1544	DJ H7^v (*)	1651	FC pl. 79 (=MG)
1551	BS p. 191 (=DJ)	1665	RS pl. 79 (≐FC)
1565	CP p. 106 (≐BS)	1666	FB p. 113 (+MG)
1566	VS fab. 60 (≐BS)		

26. *Birds, Beasts, & Bat*

A bat hovering above birds and beasts angrily facing one another.

1461	AP p. 61 (*)	1651	FC pl. 29 (=MG)
[1480?]	JZ g6^r (+AP)	1665	RS pl. 29 (=FC,
1544	DJ Fi^v (=JZ)		MG)
1564	BS p. 158 (=DJ)	1666	FB p. 61 (=MG,
1565	CP p. 191 (≐BS)		VS)
1566	VS fab. 149 (≐BS)		
1567	MG p. 104 (=BS, VS)		

Birds' Parliament. See *Peacock & Other Birds.*

Boar. See *Sow.*

Naked Body. See *Belly & Members.*

Bull. See also *Ox.*

27. *Bull & Goat (Ram)*

A bull fighting a goat (ram); a lion nearby.

1461	AP p. 116 (*)	1566	VS fab. 177 (≐JZ)
[1480?]	JZ n7^r (*)	1567	MG p. 50 (+VS)

28. *Bull & Mouse*
A bull facing a mouse.
[1480?] JZ o5^v (*)
1567   MG p. 150   (*)

Wanton Calf. See *Ox & Calf.*

29. *Camel & Flea (Fly)*
A loaded camel meeting a flea; or with a dragonfly riding
on the pack.
[1480?] JZ i7^v (*)
1668   [FB] engr. opp. p.
       61   (*)

30. *Capons, Fat & Lean*
A man and woman approaching several cocks; a thin one
standing apart.
1668   WH opp. p. 14   (*)

31. *Carter & Horse*
See also *Hercules & Carter.*
A carter beating a horse pulling a loaded cart in a
stream.
1578   MG p. 1   (*)

32. *Cat & Cock*
A cat seizing a cock.

[1480?] JZ miii^v (*)   1651   FC pl. 74   (=MG)
1544   DJ H8^v (=JZ)   1665   WH pl. 74   ($\doteq$MG)
1551   BS p. 128   (=DJ)   1666   FB p. 115   (=FC?,
1565   CP p. 69   ($\doteq$BS)   bkgr.=MG)
1566   VS fab. 6   ($\doteq$BS)
1567   MG p. 170   ($\doteq$VS
       or BS)

Cat & Mice in Bin. See *Mice & Weasel.*

33. *Cat & Mice with Petition*
Mice presenting a petition to a cat; in background a cat catching mice.

1651   FC pl. 75   (*)   1665   WH pl. 75   (≐FC)

34. *Cat, Belling of*
A cat, a bell, and mice.

1563   V. Luchino, *Faerno*   1666   FB p. 43   (*)
     pl. 47   (*)

35. *Cat (s), Fox, & Dogs*
A fox attacked by dogs (and hunter); one or more cats in a tree.

[1480?]   JZ kiiij^r (*)   1665   WH pl. 57   (=FC)
1567   MG p. 78   (+JZ)   1666   FB p. 41   (+MG)
1651   FC pl. 57   (=MG)

Cedar & Shrub. See *Woodsman, Tree, & Shrub*.

36. *Chameleon*
A hedgehoglike creature or a lizardlike one.

1534   C. Wechel, *Alciati* p.   1565   C. Plantin, *Alciati* p.
    93   (*)   158   (*)
1540   C. Wechel, *Alciati* p.   1567   MG p. 72   (+CP
    190   (+CW 1534)   *Alciati*)
1547   BS, *Alciati* p. 91
    (=CW 1540)

Clown. See *Countryman, Woodsman*.

37. *Cock & Gem*
A cock examining a gem on a dunghill.
See pls. 6–13.

[1480?]   JZ diii^r (*)   1651   FC pl. 1   (+MG)
1544   DJ A4^v (≐JZ)   1665   WH pl. 1   (≐MG,
1564   BS p. 124   (≐DJ)   FC)
1565   CP p. 171   (≐BS)   1666   FB p. 3   (+MG,
1566   VS fab. 151   (≐BS)   FC)
1567   MG p. 46   (≐BS)

Cock & Precious Stone. See *Cock & Gem.*

38. *Cocks & Partridge*
Two cocks facing one another hostilely; in background a
bird watching them.

1501	SB² [K8ᵛ]	(*)	1566	VS fab. 10 (≑BS)
1544	DJ Liᵛ	(*)	1567	MG p. 92 (≑VS)
1551	BS p. 133	(≑DJ)	1666	FB p. 179 (≑MG)
1565	CP p. 73	(≑BS)		

Countryman & Cart. See *Hercules & Carter.*

39. *Countryman & Swallow*
A swallow flying about a farmer sowing seed; other birds
watching.

1461	AP p. 30	(*)	1564	BS p. 139 (=DJ)
[1480?]	JZ e6ʳ	(+AP)	1566	VS fab. 52 (≑BS)
1544	DJ C7ᵛ	(=JZ)	1666	FB p. 37 (=VS)

40. *Countryman, Calf, & Dogs*
See also *Ox & Calf.*

A countryman about to slaughter a calf; two dogs
running away.

1501	SB² G7ᵛ	(*)	1565	CP p. 82 (≑BS)
1544	DJ Hiiiiᵛ	(*)	1566	VS fab. 23 (≑BS)
1551	BS p. 148	(=DJ)	1567	MG p. 164 (=VS)

41. *Countryman, Ox, & Wolf*
A wolf facing a countryman with an ox and plow; a dog;
in background three other scenes.

1668 [FB] engr. opp. p.
     86 (*)

42. *Countrymen & Birds in Grain*
Two harvesters; birds (larks) in field of grain.

1501	SB² Biiijʳ	(*)	1665	[RS] pl. 77 (=FC)
1571	BS p. 470	(*)	1666	FB p. 13 (=FC)
1651	FC pl. 77	(*)		

43. *Two Crabs (Crayfish)*
Mother crab or crayfish and a young one on the bank of a river or in it.

1461 AP p. 98 (*)	1578 MG p. 25 (+VS)
[1480?] JZ niii^v (=AP)	1668 WH opp. p. 20 (*)
1566 VS fab. 70 (≐AP)	

Crayfish. See *Crabs*.

44. *Crow & Pitcher*
A crow dropping a pebble in a water bucket or pitcher.

[1480?] JZ oiiij^r (*)	1668 WH opp. p. "59"
1566 VS fab. 120 (≐JZ)	[67] (=VS, FB) (in
1666 FB p. 79 (*)	background: *Eagle,*
	Crow, & Sheep, no.
	63)

45. *Crow & Scorpion*
A crow with a scorpion in its beak.

1531 H. Steyner, *Alciati* D7^v (*)	1565 C. Plantin, *Alciati* p. 136 (≐BS)
1534 C. Wechel, *Alciati* p. 78 (≐HS 1531)	1567 MG p. 198 (≐BS or CP *Alciati*)
1547 BS, *Alciati* p. 77 (*)	

46. *Crow & Sheep*
See also *Eagle, Crow, & Sheep*.

A crow on the back of a grazing sheep; no human figures.

[1480?] JZ i8^v (*)	1566 VS fab. 99 (≐BS)
1544 DJ Iii^v (+JZ)	1567 MG p. 38 (≐VS)
1564 BS p. 187 (+DJ)	

47. *Cupid & Death*
Cupid and Death shooting arrows at aged and young.

1531 H. Steyner, *Alciati* D3^v (*)	1547 BS, *Alciati* p. 67 (*)
1534 C. Wechel, *Alciati* p. 69 (=HS 1531)	1565 C. Plantin, *Alciati* p. 122 (≐BS 1547)

(cont. on p. 88)

1651   FC pl. 39   (=CP *Al-*   1665   [RS] pl. 39   (≐FC)
        ciati 1565)   1666   FB p. 123   (*)

48. *Cupid, Death, & Reputation*
Cupid and Death drinking with a figure wearing mail made of small shields.

1651   FC pl. 61   (*)
1665   RS pl. 61   (≐FC)

Deer. See *Stag.*

49. *Devil & Malefactor*
A prisoner praying to a devil.

1651   FC pl. 63   (*)
1665   RS pl. 63   (≐FC)

50. *Dog & Clog*
A dog wearing a wooden clog surrounded by other dogs.

1666   FB p. 51   (*)

51. *Old Dog & Master Hunting*
A man on foot lifting a stick to strike a hound as they pursue a stag or hare.

1461   AP p. 47   (*)   1567   MG p. 16   (=VS)
[1480?] JZ fiijʳ   (=AP)   1651   FC pl. 18   (*)
1544   DJ D5ᵛ   (*)   1665   WH pl. 18   (≐MG)
1564   BS p. 146   (=DJ)   1666   FB p. 129   (+FC)
1566   VS fab. 63   (≐BS)

52. *Dog & Ox*
A dog in a manger facing at least one ox.

[1480?] JZ lijʳ   (*)   1567   MG p. 144   (≐BS)
1544   DJ Iiᵛ   (=JZ)   1666   FB p. 59   (+MG)
[1571   BS p. 273   (≐DJ)]   1668   WH opp. p. 4
1565   CP p. 203   (≐BS)   (=MG)
1566   VS fab. 174   (≐JZ)

53. Dog & Reflection

A dog with meat in his mouth wading or swimming in a stream or standing on a plank above it; his reflection.

1461	AP p. 9 (*)		1566	VS fab. 153 (≐BS)
[1480?]	JZ d5ʳ (≐AP)		1567	MG p. 22 (=DJ)
1544	DJ Biiiᵛ (+JZ)		1651	FC pl. 2 (+VS?)
[1571	BS p. 213 (*)]		1665	WH pl. 2 (≐MG)
1565	CP p. 163 (≐BS)		1666	FB p. 161 (=MG)

54. Dog & Thief

A man offering food to a dog in or above a doorway or outside a house.

1461	AP p. 42 (*)		1566	VS fab. 129 (≐BS)
[1480?]	JZ fjʳ (≐AP)		1567	MG p. 114 (≐VS)
1544	DJ Diiᵛ (+JZ)		1651	FC pl. 21 (+MG)
1564	BS p. 143 (=DJ)		1665	WH pl. 21 (≐MG)
1565	CP p. 183 (≐BS)			

55. Dog & Wolf (I)

A dog in the company of a wolf.

[1480?]	JZ h5ʳ (*)		1566	VS fab. 35 (≐BS)
1544	DJ Hiiiᵛ (=JZ)		1666	FB p. 195 (≐VS)
1551	BS p. 162 (≐DJ)		1668	[FB] opp. p. 111
1565	CP p. 194 (≐BS)			(*)

56. Dog & Wolf (II)

A dog dressed as a steward facing a wolf; in background a wolf in a storeroom begging a steward for protection.

1668   [FB] opp. p. 113   (*)

57. Dolphin (& Tuna)

A dolphin in shallow water or on shore; sometimes also a tuna swimming or on shore.

1531	H. Steyner, *Alciati* D7ᵛ (*)		1565	C. Plantin, *Alciati* p. 138 (≐BS 1547)
1534	C. Wechel, *Alciati* p. 79 (≐HS 1531)		1577	C. Plantin, *Alciati* p. 538 (≐GR 1549)
1547	BS, *Alciati* p. 78 (=CW 1534)		1666	FB p. 207 (=CP *Alciati* 1565 or 1577)
1549	G. Rouille, *Alciati* p. 202 (=BS 1547)			

Dragon. See *Snake & File.*

58. *Dragon & Elephant*
A dragon grasping the trunk of an elephant, its tail
wound around one of the elephant's legs.

1567   MG p. 90   (*)

59. *Eagle & Fox*
A vixen setting fire to a tree (or nest) to which an eagle
has taken a fox pup.

1461	AP p. 21	(*)	1567	MG p. 84 (=JZ,
[1480?]	JZ ej^v	(≐AP)		VS)
1544	DJ H6^v	(=JZ)	1570	BS p. 119 (*)
1561	JdeM p. 186	(≐DJ	1666	FB p. 21 (+MG)
	[BS?])		1668	[FB] opp. p. 117
1566	VS fab. 172			(≐FB 1666)
	(≐JdeM [BS?])			

60. *Eagle & Other Birds*
An eagle crowned and surrounded by predators with
spears; (below) peaceful birds.

1501   SB^2 A6^v (*)
1668   [FB] engr. opp. p.
          99   (*)

61. *Eagle & Tortoise (Snail)*
An eagle carrying a tortoise or snail over a harbor or a
terrestrial globe.

1551	BS p. 193	(*)	1651	FC pl. 54 (+MG)
1566	VS fab. 61	(≐BS)	1665	WH pl. 54 (≐FC)
1567	MG p. 160	(+VS)	1666	FB p. 221 (≐VS)

Note: An eagle carrying a tortoise over birds on the ground (JZ niij^r and
VS fab. 157) is another motif.

62. *Eagle, Beetle, & Hare*
A beetle facing a hare as an eagle descends or pounces on
the hare.

[1480?]	JZ mij^v	(*)	1651	FC pl. 56 (*)
1564	BS p. 224	(*)	1665	WH pl. 56 (≐FC)
1566	VS fab. 2	(≐JZ)		

63. *Eagle, Crow, & Sheep*

See also *Crow & Sheep*.

One or two boys or a man reaching for a crow on the back of a sheep; an eagle carrying a lamb aloft.

[1480?] JZ mij^r (*)
1544 DJ Iz [K]iiii^v
    (=JZ)
1564 BS p. 186 (+DJ)
1565 CP p. 160 ($\doteq$BS)
1566 VS fab. 49 ($\doteq$BS)
1567 MG p. 154 ($\doteq$VS)
1651 FC pl. 80 (+MG?)
1665 WH pl. 80 ($\doteq$FC)

1666 FB p. 183 (+MG)
1668 WH opp. p. "59"
    [67] ($\doteq$ part of WH
    pl. 80 1665 reduced)
    WH opp. p. 93 (repeat WH pl. 80 1665)

64. *Eagle, Snail (Oyster), & Crow (Daw)*

See also *Eagle & Tortoise (Snail)*.

In the air an eagle carrying a snail or oyster; on the ground beside a rock, a smaller bird.

1461 AP p. 23 (*)
[1480?] JZ eij^r ($\doteq$AP)
1544 DJ Ci^v (=JZ)
1564 BS p. 133 (+DJ)
1565 CP p. 66 ($\doteq$BS)
1566 VS fab. 96 ($\doteq$BS)

1567 MG p. 54 ($\doteq$VS)
1651 FC pl. 4 (+MG?)
1665 WH pl. 4 ($\doteq$FC)
1668 WH opp. p. 81 (repeat WH pl. 4 1665)

Farmer. See *Countryman*.

Fir & Shrub. See *Woodsman, Tree, & Shrub*.

Fisherman. See *Angler*.

Fowler. See *Birdcatcher; Snake & Archer*.

65. *Tailless Fox*

A tailless fox surrounded by other foxes.

1544 DJ Iz [K]7^v (*)
    [Perry, p. 424]
1551 BS p. 130 (=DJ)
1565 CP p. 70 ($\doteq$BS)

1566 VS fab. 7 ($\doteq$BS)
1578 MG p. 67 (=VS)
1666 FB p. 133 (+VS)

66. *Fox & Bramblebush*
A fox in a thicket pursued by one hunter and dogs.

[1480?] JZ miiii^r (*)   1566 VS fab. 127 (≐BS)
1544 DJ Iz [K]8^v (*)   1668 WH opp. p. 16
1564 BS p. 229 (=DJ)   (+VS)
1565 CP p. 71 (≐BS)

67. *Fox & Cock*
A fox looking up at a cock in a tree.

[1480?] JZ kiii^r (*)   1651 FC pl. 49 (+VS)
[1570 BS p. 166 (*)]   1665 WH pl. 49 (≐FC)
1566 VS fab. 36 (≐JZ)   1666 FB p. 15 (=FC)

68. *Fox & Crow*
A fox looking up at a bird in a tree with a round object in
its mouth.

[1480?] JZ eiii^r (*)   1651 FC pl. 5 (≐MG)
1544 DJ Cii^v (=JZ)   1665 WH pl. 5 (≐FC)
1564 BS p. 134 (=DJ)   1666 FB p. 135 (=MG)
1565 CP p. 157 (≐BS)   1668 WH opp. p. 18 (re-
1566 VS fab. 158 (≐BS)   peat WH pl. 5 1665)
1567 MG p. 142 (=VS)

69. *Fox & Flies*
A fox in the mud attacked by flies; a hedgehog or another
fox watching.

1563 V. Luchino, *Faerno*
          pl. 17 (*)
1578 MG p. 28 (*)

70. *Fox & Grapes*
A fox beneath a grape vine.

[1480?] JZ ij^v (*)   1578 MG p. 63 (=VS)
1566 VS fab. 8 (=JZ)   1666 FB p. 187 (=MG)

71. *Fox & Hare*
A seated fox facing a seated hare.

1567 MG p. 128 (*)

72. *Fox & Porcupine*
A fox facing a porcupine.
1668   WH opp. p. 9   (*)

73. *Fox & Stork (Crane)*
A stork or crane drinking from a tall narrow-necked receptacle, while a fox licks the outside; sometimes a fox and stork or crane eating from a flat surface.

[1480?] JZ f6ᵛ (*)	1567 MG p. 180 (≐VS)	
1544 DJ Eiiᵛ (=JZ)	1651 FC pl. 26 (+MG)	
1564 BS p. 151 (+DJ)	1665 [RS] pl. 26 (≐FC)	
1565 CP p. 186 (≐BS)	1666 FB p. 171 (+MG)	
1566 VS fab. 165 (≐BS)		

74. *Fox in Well & Wolf*
A wolf looking down at a fox in a well.
(1480?]   JZ p7ʳ   (*)
1666   FB p. 17   (*)

75. *Frog & Fox.*
A frog facing a fox and other animals.

1461 AP p. 101 (*)	1666 FB p. 9 (*)
[1480?] JZ niiijʳ (+AP)	

76. *Frog, Mouse, & Kite (I)*
A frog towing a mouse on its back in water; a kite (eagle) striking or carrying mouse and kite away.

1461 AP p. 6 (*)	1566 VS fab. 152
[1480?] JZ diiiiʳ (≐AP)	(≐JdeM [BS?])
1544 DJ Biiᵛ (*)	1567 MG p. 44 (≐VS)
1561 JdeM p. 128 (≐DJ [BS?])	

77. *Frog, Mouse & Kite (II)*
A kite descending on a combat between the leaders of armies of frogs and mice.

1651 FC pl. 6 (*)	1666 FB p. 71 (≐FC)
1665 [RS] pl. 6 (≐FC)	

78. *Frogs' Assembly*

An outdoor meeting of frogs in human dress being addressed by one of their number in the Damm, Amsterdam, before "the new State-House," later the Royal Palace.

1665 WH opp. p. 207 (*)

79. *Geese & Cranes*

See also *Birdcatcher, Storks, & Geese.*
A man beating geese in grain; cranes flying away.

1666 FB p. 159 (*) [Per-
ry, p. 466]

Goat & Wolf. See *Wolf & Kid.*

80. *Goat & Wolf Cub*

A goat suckling a wolf cub.

1531	H. Steyner, *Alciati* E5ᵛ (*)	1549	G. Rouille, *Alciati* p. 87 (=BS)
1534	C. Wechel, *Alciati* p. 96 (=HS 1531)	1565	C. Plantin, *Alciati* p. 162 (≐BS 1547)
1547	BS, *Alciati* p. 94 (≐CW 1534)	1567	MG p. 186 (=GR 1548)

81. *Goat in Well & Fox*

A fox jumping out of a well from the horns of a goat or looking down at a goat in a well.
See pls. 14–21.

[1480?]	JZ miijʳ (*)	1567	MG p. 184 (+VS)
1544	DJ Iz[K]viᵛ (*)	1651	FC pl. 58 (*)
1551	BS p. 125 (+DJ)	1665	WH pl. 58 (≐FC)
1565	CP p. 67 (≐BS)	1666	FB p. 121 (=MG)
1566	VS fab. 4 (≐BS)		

82. *Hares & Frogs*

Several hares beside water; frogs jumping in.

1461	AP p. 38 (*)	1564	BS p. 110 (=DJ)
[1480?]	JZ fiijᵛ (=AP)	1565	CP p. 103 (≐BS)
1544	DJ D6ᵛ (*)	1566	VS fab. 19 (≐BS)

| 1567 | MG p. 64 | (=VS) | 1665 | WH pl. 19 | (=FC) |
| 1651 | FC pl. 19 | (=MG) | 1666 | FB p. 83 | (+MG) |

Hart. See *Stag.*

83. *Hawk & Cuckoo*
A hawk facing a smaller bird; a hanged bird.

| 1651 | FC fab. 43 | (*) |
| 1665 | [RS] fab. 43 | (=FC) |

Hawk and Doves, apparently, indoors. See *Vulture (Hawk) & Other Birds.*

84. *Hawk & Nightingale*
A hawk facing a nightingale or holding one.

[1480?]	JZ g6ᵛ	(*)	1651	FC pl. 78	(*)
1566	VS fab. 3	(+JZ)	1665	WH pl. 78	(≐FC)
1567	MG p. 148	(*)	1666	FB p. 153	(+MG)

85. *Hawk, Doves, & Kite*
Outdoors, a hawk (or kite) attacking doves beside a cote; a kite (or hawk) watching or in air with dove.

1461	AP p. 35	(*)	1567	MG p. 24	(=VS)
[1480?]	JZ e8ᵛ	(=AP)	1651	FC pl. 20	(=MG)
1544	DJ Diᵛ	(=JZ)	1665	RS pl. 20	(≐FC)
1564	BS p. 142	(=DJ)	1666	FB p. 209	(=MG?)
1566	VS fab. 101	(≐BS)			

Hawklike birds. See also *Eagle, Kite, Vulture.*

Hedgehog. See *Fox & Porcupine; Snake(s) & Porcupine.*

86. *Hen, Chicks, & Birds of Prey*
A hen guarding chicks under a basket from hawks.

| 1567 | MG p. 18 | (*) |

87.   *Hercules & Carter*

A carter lying on the ground imploring Hercules (in sky)
for aid in freeing his mired cart.

1563	V. Luchino; *Faerno*	1665	[RS] pl. 41 ($\doteq$FC)
	pl. 91 (*)	1666	FB p. 107 (=FC)
1651	FC pl. 41 (*)		

Hermes. See Mercury.

88.   *Horse & Ass (I)*

A laden ass on the ground; his master with a stick or
whip; an unbridled horse; or master transferring a load to
the horse.

1501	SB² E8ʳ (*)	1665	[RS] pl. 48 ($\doteq$FC)
1544	DJ G7ᵛ (*)	1666	FB p. 201 ($\doteq$MG,
1551	BS p. 247 (=DJ)		=VS)
1565	CP p. 97 ($\doteq$BS)	1668	[FB] opp. p. 101
1566	VS fab. 125 ($\doteq$BS)		(+FB? Pedlar & Ass)
1567	MG p. 86 (=VS)		
1651	FC pl. 48 (*)		

89.   *Horse & Ass (II)*

A horse with ornate saddle and trappings meeting an ass
carrying a sack or firewood.

1461	AP p. 73 (*)	1566	VS fab. 58 ($\doteq$BS)
[1480?]	JZ g5ʳ ($\doteq$AP)	1567	MG p. 192 (=VS)
1547	BS E8ᵛ (=JZ) [re-	1651	FC pl. 35 (+MG)
	produced in Mortimer,	1665	[RS] pl. 35 ($\doteq$FC)
	p. 6 (1551, p. 189)]	1666	FB p. 29 (=JZ)
1565	CP p. 104 ($\doteq$BS)		

90.   *Horse & Ass (III)*

A horse with an ornate saddle and trappings meeting an
ass.

1544	DJ Iz[K]iiᵛ (*)	
1578	MG p. 117 (=DJ)	

91. *Horse, Cart, & Ass (I)*
A horse drawing a cart meeting an unburdened ass.

1461   AP p. 74   (*)
1544   DJ Eviii^v (+AP?)
1578   MG p. 117 (back-
          ground)   (=DJ)

92. *Horse, Ass, & Carts (II)*
A horse hauling an empty cart meets an ass pulling a
heavily laden one.

1578   MG p. 65   (*)

Hound. See *Dog.*

Husbandman. See *Countryman.*

Jove. See *Jupiter.*

93. *Juno, Peacock, & Nightingale*
Juno standing facing a peacock, a bird in a tree; or, a
peacock facing a bird, Juno in a cloud.

[1480?]   JZ iij^v (*)   1666   FB p. 155   (=MG)
1544   DJ Iiii^v (=JZ)   1668   WH opp. p. 1
1564   BS p. 188   (*)   (+FB)
1567   MG p. 8   (=BS)

94. *Jupiter & Apes*
An ape, attended by other animals, presenting a young
ape to Jupiter enthroned.

[1480?]   JZ n7^v (*)
1566   VS p. 176   ($\doteq$JZ)
1668   WH opp. p. 104   (*)

95. *Jupiter & Bee*
A bee in the air before Jupiter enthroned.

[1480?]   JZ m7^v (*)   1566   VS p. 104   ($\doteq$BS)
1544   DJ M8^v (*)   1567   MG p. 204   (+VS)
1564   BS p. 267   ($\doteq$DJ)   1668   [FB] engr. opp. p.
1565   CP p. 205   ($\doteq$BS)   43   (+MG)

96. *Jupiter & Camel*
Jupiter on a throne or in the sky addressed by a camel.

[1480?] JZ n5ᵛ (*)   1668 [FB] engr. opp. p. 61
1566 VS fab. 179 (≐JZ)   (in background)
1666 FB p. 131 (*)   (+FB)

97. *Jupiter & Frogs*
Jupiter on the ground or in the sky, usually holding a log;
frogs in a pool and on a log; a crane spearing a frog.

1461 AP p. 33 (*)   1566 VS fab. 162 (≐BS)
[1480?] JZ e7ᵛ (*)   1567 MG p. 36 (≐VS)
1544 DJ C8ᵛ (+JZ)   1651 FC pl. 12 (=MG)
1564 BS p. 141 (=DJ)   1665 WH pl. 12 (≐FC)
1565 CP p. 236 (≐BS)   1666 FB p. 73 (*)

98. *Jupiter & Snake*
A snake offering a rose to Jupiter in the sky with other
gods.

1544 DJ N8ᵛ (*) [Perry,   1566 VS fab. 105 (≐BS)
      p. 464]   1567 MG p. 14 (=VS)
1564 BS p. 116 (+DJ)

99. *Two Kites*
Two kites facing one another, one usually lying on its
back in a nest.

1461 AP p. 29 (*)   1566 VS fab. 77 (≐JZ)
[1480?] JZ e5ᵛ (≐AP)   1567 MG p. 182 (=BS)
1544 DJ C6ᵛ (*)   1651 FC pl. 17 (≐MG)
1564 BS p. 259 (≐DJ)   1665 WH pl. 17 (≐FC)
1565 CP p. 140 (≐BS)   1666 FB p. 151 (=MG)

Laborer. See *Man, Countryman*.

Larks in Corn. See *Countrymen & Birds (Larks) in
Grain*.

100. *Leopard & Fox*
A leopard and a fox facing one another.

1666 FB p. 117 (*) [Per-
      ry, p. 423]

101. *Leopard, Stag, & Fox*
See also *Lion, Stag, & Other Beasts.*
A leopard with its foot on a dead stag facing a fox; in background an ass lying on its back; a leopard, fox, and ass chasing a stag.

1668   WH opp. p. 6
       (+[RS] 1665 *Lion,*
       Stag, & Other Beasts)

Lion & Ass. See *Ass & Boar (Lion).*

102. *Lion & Bulls*
A lion observing several bulls.

1566   VS fab. 159   (*)
       [Perry, p. 59]
1666   FB p. 7   (+VS?)

103. *Lion & Fox (I)*
A lion and a fox facing one another.

1544	DJ H5ᵛ	(*)	1567	MG p. 20 (=VS)
1551	BS p. 127	(≐DJ)	1651	FC pl. 76 (*)
1565	CP p. 68	(≐BS)	1665	WH pl. 76 (≐FC)
1566	VS fab. 5	(≐BS)	1666	FB p. 55 (+MG)

104. *Sick Lion & Fox (II)*
A fox looking at a lion in a den.

[1480?]	JZ i6ʳ	(*)	1651	FC pl. 38 (=MG)
1564	BS p. 93	(+JZ)	1665	WH pl. 38 (=FC)
1566	VS fab. 72	(=BS)	1666	FB p. 103 (+VS?)
1578	MG p. 2	(*)		

105. *Lion & Goat*
A goat (kid) on an outcropping of rock looking down on a lion.

1461	AP p. 135	(*)	1668 FB opp. p. 32
[1480?]	JZ oiij'ᵛ(≐AP)		(=JZ)
1566	VS fab. 64	(≐JZ)	

106.   *Doctor Lion & Horse*
See also *Old Lion, Horse,* etc.
A horse kicking a lion in the face.

1461	AP p. 71	(*)		1567	MG p. 6	(≐BS)
[1480?]	JZ giiij^v	(=AP)		1651	FC pl. 64	(+MG)
1544	DJ E7^v	(=JZ)		1665	WH pl. 64	(≐FC)
1564	BS p. 156	(=DJ)		1666	FB p. 111	(+MG)

107.   *Lion & Mouse*
A mouse on a pole gnawing a rope tied to a lion; or a mouse on the ground gnawing a rope tied to a net in which a lion is trapped.
See pls. 22–30.

1461	AP p. 27	(*)		1566	VS fab. 161	(≐BS)
[1480?]	JZ eiiij^v	(+AP)		1567	MG p. 202	(=VS)
1544	DJ C5^v	(*)		1651	FC pl. 9	(=MG)
1564	BS p. 138	(≐DJ)		1665	WH pl. 9	(≐MG)
1565	CP p. 181	(≐BS)		1666	FB p. 47	(=FC)

108.   *Lion, Ass, & Cock*
A cock crowing; an ass looking at a lion or chasing him; a lion devouring an ass.

1564	BS p. 89	(*) [Perry, p. 436]
1578	MG p. 4	(+BS)
1666	FB p. 93	(*)

109.   *Lion, Ass, & Fox*
A fox watching a lion devour an ass (sheep).

1544	DJ I7^v [Perry, p. 494]			1566	VS fab. 38	(≐BS)
				1567	MG p. 52	(=VS)
1564	BS p. 193	(+DJ)		1666	FB p. 185	(*)
1565	CP p. 92	(≐BS)				

110.   *Lion, Bear, & Fox*
A lion and bear fighting or reclining; a fox stealing their prey.

1570	BS p. 170	(*) [Perry, p. 449]		1666	FB p. 77	(*)

111. *Lion, Bear, & Other Beasts*
See also *Lion, Stag, & Other Beasts.*
A bear facing a lion, surrounded by a camel, stag, bull,
and other beasts.
1567   MG p. 10   (*)

112. *Lion, Boar, & Vulture*
A vulture watching a lion and a boar fighting.
1549   G. Rouille, *Alciati* p.
155   (*) [Perry, p.
484]
1567   MG p. 134   (≐GR
1549)

113. *Lioness & Fox*
A lioness with one cub facing a vixen with several.
1666   FB p. 65   (*) [Perry,
p. 473]

114. *Lioness & Mouse*
A lioness, attended by a lion and other animals, stepping
on a mouse.
1651   FC pl. 10   (*)
1665   WH pl. 10   (=FC)
1666   FB p. 49   (=FC)

115. *Old Lion, Horse (Ass), Bull, & Boar*
See also *Doctor Lion & Horse.*
A horse or ass kicking a recumbent lion as bull and boar
look on.

1461	AP p. 24 (*)	1567	MG p. 120 (=VSb)
[1480?]	JZ eiij^v (+AP)	1651	FC pl. 23 (=MG)
1544	DJ Ciii^v (=JZ)	1665	RS pl. 23 (≐FC)
1564	BS p. 156 (=DJ	1666	FB p. 199 (+FC)
	Doctor Lion & Horse)		
1565	CP p. 179 (≐BS)		
1566	VS (a) fab. 111		
	(≐JZ)		
	(b) fab. 114		
	(≐BS)		

116. *Lion, Man, & Daughter*
A man clipping the claws of a lion; a young woman watching; a man stabbing or spearing a lion.

[1480?] JZ l7ᵛ (*)   1665 [RS] pl. 51 ($\doteq$FC)
1651 FC pl. 51 (*)   1666 FB p. 219 (*)

117. *Lion, Man, & Sculpture*
A lion attacking a man; in background a sculpture of a man vanquishing a lion.

[1480?] JZ i7ʳ (*)   1567 MG p. 42 (+JZ,
1544 DJ Niiiᵛ (=JZ)   VS)
1564 BS p. 276 ($\doteq$DJ) 1651 FC pl. 50 (*)
1565 CP p. 151 ($\doteq$BS) 1665 WH pl. 50 ($\doteq$FC)
1566 VS fab. 185 ($\doteq$BS) 1666 FB p. 211 (+MG)

118. *Lion, Stag, & Other Beasts*
See also *Leopard, Stag, & Other Beasts; Lion, Ass, & Fox; Lion, Bear, & Other Beasts.*

A lion with a dead stag or remains of prey watched by other beasts.

1461 AP p. 13 (*)   1567 MG p. 196 (=HH)
[1480?] JZ d5ᵛ (=AP)   1651 FC pl. 3 (=MG)
1544 DJ Biiiiᵛ (*)   1665 RS pl. 3 (=FC)
1564 BS p. 128 (+DJ?)   1666 FB p. 45 (*)
1565 CP p. 143 ($\doteq$BS)
1566 HH fab. 37 (=BS)
      VS fab. 154 ($\doteq$JZ)

Lobsters. See Crabs.

119. *Old Man & Death*
An old man with a burden confronted by Death.

1544 DJ L7ᵛ (*) [Perry,   1566 VS fab. 20 ($\doteq$BS)
      p. 431]   1578 MG p. 5 (+VS)
1551 BS p. 144 (+DJ)   1666 FB p. 203 (+MG?)
1565 CP p. 80 ($\doteq$BS)

120. *Covetous Man & Envious Man*
Apollo facing two men, one with his finger to his eye; sometimes a kneeling man blinding a recumbent man.

1461   AP p. 129   (*)   1666   FB p. 167   (*)
[1480?]   JZ oii^v   (*)   1668   Josiah English opp. p.
1566   VS fab. 43   (=JZ)   40   (=FB)

121.   Man & Flea

A man in bed holding a flea in his fingers; or a man in
bed in a shed and a poor man facing three ladies dining out
of doors.

[1480?]   JZ nj^r   (*)   1668   [FB] opp. p. 78   (*)
1566   VS fab. 62   (≐JZ)

122.   Bald Man & Fly

A seated man waving flies away from his head.

1461   AP p. 56   (*)   1566   VS fab. 180   (=JZ)
[1480?]   JZ f6^r   (+AP)   1668   WH opp. p. 22   (*)

123.   Man & Goose

A man approaching one goose or also holding another
goose upside down.

1461   AP p. 119   (*)   1666   FB p. 193   (*)
[1480?]   JZ o6^r   (+AP)   1668   [FB] engr. opp. p.
1566   VS fab. 74   (≐JZ)   46   (*)

124.   Man & Idol

A man smashing a statue or looking at one already
broken, sometimes with coins scattered about.

[1480?]   JZ miiij^v   (*)   1566   VS fab. 90   (≐BS)
1544   DJ Liii^v   (=JZ)   1578   MG p. 22   (*)
1551   BS p. 257   (=DJ)   1668   [FB] opp. p. 37
1565   CP p. 137   (≐BS)   (=MG)

125.   Man & Mice

Two mice running away from a pursuing man; in
background a man sitting outdoors before a bonfire.

1567   MG p. 70   (*)

126.   Man & Three Sons

A man seated facing three young men.

[1480?]   JZ liiij^r   (*)
1666   FB p. 125   (+JZ)

127. *Mercury & Woodcutter*

Mercury, in or beside water, offering a man one, two, or three axes.

[1480?] JZ m8^r (*)	1668 [FB] opp. p. 107
1551 BS p. 173 (*)	(=VS) (in back-
1566 VS fab. 44 (≐BS)	ground two other
	scenes)

128. *Mice & Weasel (Cat)*

Mice about a weasel or a cat near sheaves of grain outdoors or in a granary bin.

1461 AP p. 105 (*)	1567 MG p. 100 (+VS)
[1480?] JZ ij^v (*)	1651 FC pl. 59 (*)
1544 DJ Iiiii^v (*)	1665 WH pl. 59 (≐FC)
1564 BS p. 188 (+DJ)	
1565 CP p. 226 (≐BS)	
1566 VS a) fab. 28	
(≐JZ)	
b) fab. 156	
(≐BS)	

129. *Mountain & Mouse*

Men watching a mouse emerge from a hole in a mountain.

1461 AP p. 45 (*)	1566 VS fab. 51 (≐BS)
[1480?] JZ fij^r (=AP)	1578 MG p. 46 (=VS)
1544 DJ Diiii^v (=JZ)	1651 FC pl. 8 (=MG)
1564 BS p. 145 (≐DJ)	1665 WH pl. 8 (≐FC)
1565 CP p. 174 (≐BS)	1666 FB p. 147 (=MG?)

130. *City Mouse & Country Mouse*

Two mice in a larder; a servant entering.
See pls. 31–38.

1461 AP p. 20 (*)	1651 FC pl. 7 (+MG)
[1480?] JZ d8^v (≐AP)	1665 WH pl. 7 (≐FC)
1544 DJ B8^v (+JZ)	1666 FB p. 35 (=BS,
1564 BS p. 132 (=DJ)	FC)
1567 MG p. 176 (+BS)	

131. *Mouse & Oyster*
Beside the sea a mouse with its head caught by an oyster;
or a mouse caught in a trap.

1531	H. Steyner, *Alciati* p. E3ᵛ (*)	1565	C. Plantin, *Alciati* p. 156 (≐BS 1547)
1534	C. Wechel, *Alciati* p. 91 (*)	1567	MG p. 138 (=BS or CP *Alciati*)
1547	BS, *Alciati* p. 89 (≐CW 1534)		

132. *Mule & Horses*
A mule in a stable; horses cavorting outside.

1544	DJ M5ᵛ (*) [Perry, p. 79]	1564	BS p. 254 (≐DJ)
		1567	MG p. 158 (≐BS)

Oak. See *Tree, Trees.*

133. *Ostrich & Nightingale*
An ostrich facing a small bird on a branch.

1567   MG p. 212 (*)

Ox. See also *Bull.*

134. *Ox & Calf*
See also *Countryman, Calf, & Dogs.*
A calf (bullock) about to be sacrificed; an ox plowing.

1544	DJ Miᵛ (*) [Perry, p. 53]	1567	MG p. 12 (=VS)
[1571	BS p. 302 (≐DJ)]	1666	FB p. 105 (*)
1561	JdeM p. 261 (≐BS)	1668	WH opp. p. 24 (+FB)
1566	VS fab. 187 (≐BS)		

135. *Ox & Frog (Toad)*
An ox facing a frog (toad).

1461	AP p. 64 (*)	1566	VS fab. 166 (≐BS)
[1480?]	JZ gijᵛ (≐AP)	1567	MG p. 32 (=VS)
1544	DJ E6ᵛ (=JZ)	1651	FC pl. 13 (=MG)
1564	BS p. 155 (=DJ)	1665	WH pl. 13 (≐FC)
1565	CP p. 190 (≐BS)	1666	FB p. 53 (=MG)

136. *Ox & Steer*
An ox facing a steer; a wolf and fox watching.
1668   WH opp. p. 30   (*)

137. *Painter & Devil*
An artist painting a portrait of the Devil in seventeenth-
century dress.
1668   [FB] engr. opp. p.
        74   (*)

138. *Panther & Shepherds*
A panther in a hole surrounded by shepherds.
[1480?]   JZ iiij^r (*)
1565   CP p. 197   (*)
1668   [FB] engr. opp. p.
        125   (+JZ) (back-
        ground: two other
        scenes)

139. *Peacock & Crane*
A crane facing a peacock.
[1480?]   JZ n8^r (*)
1566   VS fab. 182   ($\doteq$JZ)
1666   FB p. 89   (=VS)

Peacock & Nightingale. See *Juno.*

140. *Peacock & Other Birds*
A peacock surrounded by various kinds of birds.

1544	DJ I6^v (*)		1567	MG p. 96 (=BS)
1551	BS p. 183 (=DJ)		1651	FC pl. 40 (*)
1565	CP p. 101 ($\doteq$BS)		1665	RS pl. 40 ($\doteq$FC)
1566	VS fab. 53 (+BS)		1666	FB p. 33 (+MG)

141. *Peacocks & Jay (Daw)*
Peacocks or other birds surrounding a smaller bird with
peacock feathers attached to its tail.

1461	AP p. 58 (*)		1544	DJ Eiiii^v (*)
[1480?]	JZ f7^v ($\doteq$AP)		1564	BS p. 153 (=JZ)

1567 MG p. 162 (=BS) 1665 [RS] pl. 30 (≒FC)
1651 FC pl. 30 (=MG) 1666 FB p. 95 (=MG)

Peasant. See *Countryman.*

142. *Phoenix*
A phoenix standing in a burning nest.

1562 C. Plantin, *Paradin* p. 1567 MG p. 208 (+CP
55ᵛ and p. 172ᵛ (*) *Paradin*)

143. *Pine & Gourd*
A gourd plant beside a pine tree or twined about one.

1531 H. Steyner, *Alciati* 1565 C. Plantin, *Alciati* p.
D5ʳ (*) 127 (≒BS 1547)
1534 C. Wechel, *Alciati* p. 1565 C. Plantin, *Aesop* p.
72 (≒HS 1531) 223 (≒BS 1547)
1547 BS, *Alciati* p. 71 1651 FC pl. 62 (+CP)
(=CW 1534) 1665 WH pl. 62 (≒FC)

Pismire. See *Ant.*

Porcupine. See *Fox & Flies.*

144. *Two Pots*
Two pots floating in a stream.

1461 AP p. 115 (*) 1565 C. Plantin, *Alciati* p.
[1480?] JZ n6ᵛ (≒AP) 106 (≒BS 1547)
1531 H. Steyner, *Alciati* 1565 CP p. 208 (≒BS)
Diʳ (≒JZ) 1566 VS fab. 30 (≒BS)
1534 C. Wechel, *Alciati* p. 1666 FB p. 169 (+?)
62 (≒HS 1531)
1547 BS, *Alciati* p. 60
(≒CW 1534)

Rabbit. See *Hare.*

Rat. See *Mouse.*

Ringdove & Fowler. See *Snake & Archer.*

Rooster. See *Cock, Capon.*

Rustic. See *Countryman, Man.*

Rustic & Cart. See *Hercules & Cart.*

145.   *Satyr & Countryman (Traveler)*
A satyr watching a man blowing on his hands or food; sometimes a woman at a hearth.

[1480?] JZ o5ʳ (*)	1651 FC pl. 46 (=VS?)
[1570 BS p. 260 (*)]	1665 WH pl. 46 (≐FC)
1566 VS fab. 126 (≐JZ)	1666 FB p. 149 (≐MG)
1567 MG p. 60 (+BS?)	

146.   *Satyr & Sword*
A satyr holding a sword pommel up in front of him; in background women swimming.

1668   WH opp. p. 34   (*)

Serpent. See *Snake.*

147.   *Sheep & Butcher*
A man cutting a sheep's throat; rams watching.

[1480?] JZ iiijᵛ (*)	1668 [FB] opp. p. 49 (*)
1566 (?) fab. 189 (≐JZ)	

148.   *Shepherd Boy & Wolf*
A shepherd boy shouting after a wolf as it carries off a sheep.

[1480?] JZ m6ᵛ (*)	1566 VS fab. 173 (≐BS)
1544 DJ M6ᵛ (+JZ)	1567 MG p. 166 (≐VS)
1564 BS p. 118 (=DJ)	1666 FB p. 119 (=MG)
1565 CP p. 204 (≐BS)	

149.   *Smith & Dog*
A smith working at an anvil; a dog lying under a bench.

1544 DJ N6ᵛ (*) [Perry,	1564 BS p. 253 (≐DJ)
p. 499]	1567 MG p. 34 (≐BS)

150. *Snake & Archer*
See also *Snake & Birdcatcher*.
A snake biting the foot of an archer or fowler shooting at
a bird in a tree.
See pls. 39–42.

1531	H. Steyner, *Alciati* E2^v (*)	1565	C. Plantin, *Alciati* p. 152 ($\doteq$BS 1547)
1534	C. Wechel, *Alciati* p. 88 (+HS 1531)	1666	FB p. 25 (+?)
1547	BS, *Alciati* p. 86 (+CW 1534)		

151. *Snake & Birdcatcher*
See also *Snake & Archer; Birdcatcher & Bird.*
A snake biting the foot of a birdcatcher with a net; a bird
in a tree.

1501	S. Brant^2 Eiiij^r (*)	1565	CP p. 87 ($\doteq$BS)
1544	DJ Hi^v (=SB^2?)	1566	VS fab. 17 ($\doteq$BS)
1551	BS p. 159 (=DJ)	1567	MG p. 132 (+VS)

152. *Snake & Countryman (I)*
A man about to strike a snake before a kitchen fire.

1461	AP p. 17 (*)	1567	MG p. 80 ($\doteq$VS)
[1480?]	JZ d7^v (=AP)	1651	FC pl. 16 (=MG)
1544	DJ B6^v (=JZ)	1665	WH pl. 16 ($\doteq$MG,
1551	BS p. 269 ($\doteq$DJ)		FC)
1565	CP p. 146 ($\doteq$BS)	1666	FB p. 101 (*)
1566	VS fab. 141 ($\doteq$BS)		

153. *Snake & Countryman (II)*
A man about to strike a snake outdoors; sometimes a
sword on the ground; in background man and snake.

1461	AP p. 39 (*)	1566	VS fab. 155 (=BS)
[1480?]	JZ f5^r ($\doteq$AP)	1651	FC pl. 25 (=VS)
1544	DJ Ei^v (=JZ)	1665	WH pl. 25 ($\doteq$FC)
1564	BS p. 150 ($\doteq$DJ)		

154.   Snake & File
In a smithy a snake biting a file and/or a dragon biting an anvil.

[1480?]	JZ hiij^v	(*)	1651	FC pl. 27 (+MG)
1544	DJ Fiiii^v	(=JZ)	1665	WH pl. 27 (≐FC)
1564	BS p. 161	(+DJ)	1666	FB p. 91 (=MG,
1578	MG p. 24	(*)		FC)

Snake & Fowler. See *Snake & Archer.*

155.   Snake(s) & Porcupine
Snake(s) denying a porcupine (hedgehog) entrance to a den.

1567   MG p. 68   (*)   1666   FB p. 81   (=MG)

156.   Sow & Horses
A sow lying down facing a caparisoned war horse.

1567   MG p. 102   (*)

157.   Sow & Wolf
A sow with her pigs facing a wolf.

1461	AP p. 44	(*)	1566	VS fab. 68 (≐BS)
[1480?]	JZ fj^v	(=AP)	1567	MG p. 156 (=VS)
1544	DJ Diii^v	(+JZ)	1651	FC pl. 71 (≐MG)
1564	BS p. 144	(≐DJ)	1665	WH pl. 71 (≐MG)
1565	CP p. 184	(≐BS)	1666	FB p. 27 (+MG)

158.   Spider & Swallow
A spider dangling from a swallow in flight.

1651   FC pl. 60   (*)   1665   [RS] pl. 60   (≐FC)

159.   Drunken Stag
A stag collapsed on the floor; a wine bowl on a table.

1567   MG p. 56   (*)

160.   Stag & Fawn
A stag and fawn listening to a hunt in the background.

1563	V. Luchino, *Faerno*	1666	FB p. 127 (*)
	pl. 23 (*)		

161. *Stag & Horse*
A stag hunted by a mounted man with a sword or spear.

[1480?)	JZ i5ʳ (*)	1651	FC pl. 45 (+MG)
1544	DJ Liiiiᵛ (=JZ)	1665	WH pl. 45 (≐FC)
1556	BS (=DJ)	1666	FB p. 189 (=MG,
1565	CP p. 156 (≐BS)		FC)
1567	MG p. 140 (=BS)		

162. *Stag & Reflection*
A stag looking at his reflection in water; in background a hunted stag.
See pls. 43–50.

[1480?]	JZ g8ʳ (*)	1567	MG p. 122 (≐VS)
1544	DJ Fiiiᵛ (+JZ)	1651	FC pl. 28 (≐MG)
1564	BS p. 160 (+DJ)	1665	WH pl. 28 (≐MG)
1566	VS fab. 123 (≐BS)	1666	FB p. 213 (=MG?)

163. *Stag in Ox Stall*
A farmer discovering a stag hiding in an ox stall.

[1480?]	JZ h7ᵛ (*)	1567	MG p. 168 (≐VS)
1544	DJ Giᵛ (*)	1651	FC pl. 37 (=MG)
1564	BS p. 166 (+DJ)	1665	WH pl. 37 (≐MG)
1565	CP p. 195 (≐BS)	1666	FB p. 215 (=DJ,
1566	VS fab. 169 (≐BS)		MG)

164. *Stork & Young (I)*
A stork bringing a snake to its young in a nest on the ridge of a cottage roof.

1547	BS, *Alciati* p. 7 (*)	1567	MG p. 48 (=CP
1565	C. Plantin, *Alciati* p.		*Alciati*)
	8 (≐BS 1547)		

165. *Stork & Young (II)*
A stork standing over young ones in a nest on the ridge of a cottage roof.

1501	S. Brant² Ljᵛ (*)
1567	MG p. 216
	(=SB²?)

166.   *Swan & Stork*
A swan on a nest facing a stork.
1567   MG p. 200   (*)
1668   WH opp. p. 11   (*)

167.   *Tiger, Fox, & Hunter*
A hunter in ambush; a tiger wounded by an arrow; a
fox.

[1480?]   JZ n8^v (*)   1668   WH opp. p. 96
1566   VS fab. 183   (=JZ)   (+FB)
1666   FB p. 63   (*)

168.   *Tortoise & Frogs*
A tortoise facing frogs; in a stream fish eating frogs.
1651   FC pl. 53   (*)
1665   WH pl. 53   (≐FC)

169.   *Tortoise, Hare, & Fox*
A tortoise, fox, and hare facing one another.
1544   DJ N5^v (*)   1567   MG p. 178   (=VS)
1564   BS p. 279   (+DJ)   1666   FB p. 141   (=MG)
1566   VS fab. 192   (≐BS)

170.   *Tree & Reeds*
An uprooted tree (oak, ash, fir, olive) and reeds bending
in the wind.
[1480?]   JZ kj^r (*)   1578   MG p. 16   (≐VS)
1544   DJ L8^v (+JZ)   1651   FC pl. 67   (≐MG)
1551   BS p. 272   (≐DJ)   1665   WH pl. 67   (≐FC)
1565   CP p. 148   (≐BS)   1666   FB p. 67   (=MG)
1566   VS fab. 143   (≐BS)

171.   *Trees (Oak & Elm)*
One tree (an oak) in the midst of lower trees, including
an elm.
1578   MG p. 3   (*)

172. *Trumpeter Captured*
A trumpeter captured by two soldiers.

1531 H. Steyner, *Alciati* C7ᵛ (*)
1534 C. Wechel, *Alciati* p. 59 (+HS 1531)
1544 DJ Hiiᵛ (=HS 1531?)
1547 BS, *Alciati* D5ʳ (=CW 1534)

1551 BS p. 271 (BS 1547 block)
1565 CP, *Alciati* p. 100 (≐BS)
1565 CP p. 147 (≐BS)
1566 VS fab. 142 (≐BS)
1666 FB p. 177 (*)

173. *Turkey & Cock*
A turkey facing a cock.

1567 MG p. 190 (*)

Viper. See *Snake.*

174. *Vulture (Hawk) & Other Birds*
See also *Hawk, Doves, & Kite.*
A large bird biting a smaller bird on the ground; others watching outdoors or flying about indoors.

1461 AP p. 69 (*)
[1480?] JZ i6ʳ (=AP)
1544 DJ Iz[K]iiiᵛ (+JZ)

1564 BS p. 196 (=DJ)
1566 VS fab. 98 (≐BS)
1567 MG p. 188 (≐VS)

175. *Weasel & Fox*
In a larder a weasel on a shelf and a fat fox before an aperture.

1651 FC pl. 42 (*) [Perry, p. 107]
1665 WH pl. 42 (≐FC)

176. *Wind & Earthen Vessel*
An earthen vessel in a storm; or a man striving to save an earthen vessel shattered by a blast.

[1480?] JZ o6ᵛ (*)
1668 WH opp. p. 71 (*)

177. *North Wind & Sun*
One man muffled up as wind blows on him; another removing his cloak as sun beats on him.

1578   MG p. 13   (*) [Per-   1665   WH pl. 65   (≐FC)
ry, p. 29]   1666   FB p. 69   (+MG)
1651   FC pl. 65   (=MG)

178. *Wolf & Crane*
A crane with its bill in the mouth of a wolf.

1461   AP p. 16   (*)   1651   FC pl. 15   (=MG)
[1480?] JZ d6ᵛ   (≐AP)   (on plate with 14)
1544   DJ B5ᵛ   (=JZ)   1665   WH pl. 15   (=FC)
1551   BS p. 273   (≐DJ)   (on plate with 14)
1565   CP p. 149   (≐BS)   1666   FB p. 165   (=MG?)
1566   VS fab. 144   (≐BS)
1567   MG p. 136   (=VS)

179. *Wolf & Fox*
See also *Wolf, Fox, & Countryman.*
A fox facing a wolf in the mouth of a den.

[1480?] JZ g7ᵛ   (*)   1651   FC pl. 32   (=JZ)
1566   VS fab. 135   (≐JZ)   1665   WH pl. 32   (≐FC)

180. *Wolf & Head*
A wolf with an effigy or the head of a broken statue.

1461   AP p. 56   (*)   1566   VS fab. 11   (≐BS)
[1480?] JZ f7ʳ   (+AP)   1567   MG p. 28   (+VS)
1544   DJ Eiiiᵛ   (*)   1651   FC pl. 22   (≐MG)
1551   BS p. 135   (=DJ)   1665   WH pl. 22   (≐FC)
1565   CP p. 74   (≐BS)

181. *Wolf & Hedgehog*
A hedgehog facing a wolf.

1567   MG p. 94   (*) [Per-
ry, p. 579]

182. *Wolf & Kid*
See also *Wolf & Sheep (II)*.
A wolf at the door of a cottage; a kid in a side window or
door.

1461	AP p. 36	(*)	1566	VS fab. 139	(=JZ)
[1480?]	JZ fiiij^v	(≐AP)	1567	MG p. 58	(≐VS)
1544	DJ D7^v	(=JZ)	1651	FC pl. 72	(+MG)
1564	BS p. 148	(=DJ)	1665	WH pl. 72	(≐FC)
1565	CP p. 144	(≐BS)			

183. *Wolf & Lamb*
A wolf watching a lamb drink from a stream; or a wolf
and lamb standing beside a stream.

1461	AP p. 11	(*)	1566	VS fab. 106	(≐BS)
[1480?]	JZ diij^v	(≐AP)	1567	MG p. 152	(≐VS)
1544	DJ Bi^v	(=JZ)	1651	FC pl. 14	(=MG)
1551	BS p. 236	(=DJ)	1665	WH pl. 14	(=FC)
1565	CP p. 165	(≐BS)	1666	FB p. 5	(=MG)

184. *Wolf & Sheep (I)*
A sheep with a clog tied to it pursued into a house by a
wolf.

1567   MG p. 214   (*)

185. *Wolf & Sheep (II)*
See also *Wolf & Kid*.
A sheep in a side window; a wolf outside covered by a
lamb's skin.

1578   MG p. 21   (*)

186. *Wolf, Child, & Nurse*
A woman and child in a house or a yard; a wolf
watching.

1461	AP p. 97	(*)	1566	VS fab. 73	(=JZ)
[1480?]	JZ nij^v	(+AP)	1666	FB p. 139	(*)

187. *Wolf, Fox, & Countryman*
See also *Wolf & Fox.*
A man with a club or pole attacking a wolf before its den;
a fox watching or running away or both.

[1480?]	JZ iijʳ	(*)		1567	MG p. 88	(=BS)
1544	DJ Fijᵛ	(*)		1666	FB p. 85	(≐MG)
1564	BS p. 159	(=DJ)				

188. *Wolf, Fox, & Trout*
A wolf and fox facing one another above a trout; men
beating a wolf dragging a basket of stones; in background a
wolf and lion king.

1668   [FB] opp. p. 52   (*)
       Fables XXI, XXII,
       and XXIII

189. *Wolf in Sheep's Skin*
Two shepherds looking at a wolf covered by a sheep's
skin hanging from a tree.

1567   MG p. 194   (*)
       [Perry, p. 513]
1666   FB p. 23   (=MG)

190. *Wolf, Kites, Sheep, & Dog*
A wolf facing a dog and sheep; two kites watching.

1544	DJ Giiiiᵛ	(*)		1651	FC pl. 81	(*)
1564	BS p. 172	(=DJ)		1665	WH pl. 81	(≐FC)
1566	VS fab. 1	(≐BS)		1666	FB p. 87	(=MG)
1567	MG p. 98	(≐VS)				

191. *Wolf, Lamb, & Goat*
A wolf facing a lamb and goat.

1461	AP p. 46	(*)		1567	MG p. 124	(≐BS)
[1480?]	JZ fijᵛ	(+AP)		1651	FC pl. 66	(=MG)
1544	DJ G5ᵛ	(=JZ)		1665	WH pl. 66	(≐FC)
1564	BS p. 173	(≐DJ)		1666	FB p. 31	(≐FC)

192. *Wolf, Sheep, & Stag*
A wolf facing a sheep and a stag.

1461	AP p. 40	(*)	1565	CP p. 185 (≐BS)
[1480?]	JZ f5ᵛ	(≐AP)	1566	VS fab. 163 (≐BS)
1544	DJ D8ᵛ	(=JZ)	1567	MG p. 118 (≐VS)
1564	BS p. 149	(≐DJ)		

193. *Wolves & Sheep*
Wolves attacking sheep; shepherds.

1461	AP p. 138	(*)	1566	VS fab. 148
[1480?]	JZ m6ᵛ	(+AP)		(≐JdeM [BS?])
1544	DJ F5ᵛ	(*)	1567	MG p. 76 (+VS)
1561	JdeM p. 164	(=DJ	1651	FC pl. 31 (=MG)
	[BS?])		1665	WH pl. 31 (≐FC)
1565	CP p. 111	(≐[BS?])	1666	FB p. 19 (+MG)

194. *Woman & Cock (I)*
A woman about to cut a cock's throat.

1544	DJ Niiᵛ	(*)	1566	VS fab. 24 (≐BS)
1551	BS p. 149	(≐DJ)	1567	MG p. 66 (=VS)
1565	CP p. 83	(≐BS)		

195. *Women & Cock (II)*
Old woman; her two maids about to kill a cock.

[1480?]	JZ g8ᵛ	(*)	1566	VS fab. 15 (≐BS)
1544	DJ Iz[K]iᵛ	(*)	1666	FB p. 75 (*)
1551	BS p. 209	(*)		

196. *Woodsman & Trees (I)*
A man (men) chopping a tree in a forest.

[1480?]	JZ hiiijᵛ	(*)	1578	MG p. 57 (≐VS)
1544	DJ F6ᵛ	(=JZ)	1651	FC pl. 36 (=MG)
[1571	BS p. 256	(≐DJ)]	1665	WH pl. 36 (≐FC)
1565	CP p. 193	(≐BS)	1666	FB p. 197 (=MG)
1566	VS fab. 82	(≐BS)		

197. *Woodsman, Tree, & Shrub (II)*
A woodsman chopping a tree beside a shrub.

1461   AP p. 126   (*)
[1480?]   JZ oj^v ($\doteq$AP)
1668   WH opp. p. 84   (*)

198. *Youth & Cat*
A youth kneeling and holding a cat or the hand of a young woman with the lower half of a cat; (above) Venus and Cupid.

1544	DJ G6^v (*)	1651	FC pl. 73 (*)
1564	BS p. 58 (*)	1665	WH pl. 73 ($\doteq$FC)
1565	CP p. 155 ($\doteq$BS)	1666	FB p. 143 (=VS,
1566	VS fab. 171 ($\doteq$BS)		FC)

199. *Youth & Swallow*
A barelegged youth before a dead swallow on the ground.

1544	DJ Ni^v (*)	1567	MG p. 82 ($\doteq$BS)
1564	BS p. 269 ($\doteq$DJ)	1666	FB p. 191 ($\doteq$MG)

Zeus. See *Jupiter.*

Plates

10. Plates

Each book is understood to be an *Aesop* unless it is said to be an *Alciati*. When known, the artist is named, then the printer, and, when other than London, the place of publication. When a reproduction is not taken from the first edition, the date of the edition from which it is taken is noted in italics.

Pl.   1   1531. *Alciati*. Anon. H. Steyner,
         Augsburg.

Pl.   2   1534. *Alciati*. Anon. C. Wechel,
         Paris.

Pl.   3   1547. *Alciati*. B. Salomon.
         J. de Tournes, Lyons.

Pl. 4 1567. *1578*. M. Gheeraerts. P. de Clerck for M. Gheeraerts, Bruges.

Pl. 5 1666. F. Barlow. W. Godbid for F. Barlow.

Pl. 6   [ca. 1476]. [*1480?*]. Anon. J. Zainer, Ulm.

Pl. 7   1542. *1544*. Anon. D. Ja-   Pl. 8   1561. Anon. J. de Mar-
            not, Paris.   nef, Paris.

Pl. 9   1566. V. Solis. S. Feyerabend, Frankfort.

Pl. 10   1567. *1578*. M. Gheeraerts. P. de Clerck for M. Gheeraerts, Bruges.

Pl. 11   1651. F. Cleyn. T. Warren for A. Crook.

Pl. 12   1665. W. Hollar. T. Roycroft for J. Ogilby.

Pl. 13   1666. F. Barlow. W. Godbid for F. Barlow.

Pl. 14   [ca. 1476]. [*1480?*]. Anon. J. Zainer, Ulm.

Pl. 15   1542. *1544*. Anon. D. Janot, Paris.

Pl. 16   1551. *1570*. B. Salomon.   J.   de
Tournes, Lyons.

Pl. 17   1566. V. Solis. S. Feyerabend, Frankfort.

Pl. 18   1567. *1578*. M. Gheeraerts. P. de Clerck for M. Gheeraerts, Bruges.

Pl. 19   1651. F. Cleyn. T. Warren for A. Crook.

Pl. 20   1665. W. Hollar. T. Roycroft for J. Ogilby.

Pl. 21   1666. F. Barlow. W. Godbid for F. Barlow.

Pl. 22　1461. *1908*. Anon. A. Pfister, Bamberg.

Pl. 23　[ca. 1476]. [*1480?*]. Anon. J. Zainer, Ulm.

Pl. 24   1542. *1544*. Anon. D. Janot, Paris.

Pl. 25   1561. Anon. J. de Marnef, Paris.

Pl. 26   1566. V. Solis. S. Feyerabend, Frankfort.

Pl. 27   1567. *1578*. M. Gheeraerts. P. de Clerck for M. Gheer-
         aerts, Bruges.

Pl. 28   1651. F. Cleyn. T. Warren for A. Crook.

Pl. 29   1665. W. Hollar. T. Roycroft for J. Ogilby.

Pl. 30   1666. F. Barlow. W. Godbid for F. Barlow.

Pl. 31   1461. *1908*. Anon. A. Pfister, Bamberg.

Pl. 32   [ca. 1476]. [*1480?*]. Anon. J. Zainer, Ulm.

Pl. 33   1542. *1544*. Anon. D. Ja-
           not, Paris.

Pl. 34   1561. Anon. J. de Mar-
           nef, Paris.

Pl. 35   1567. *1578*. M. Gheeraerts. P. de Clerck for M. Gheer-
         aerts, Bruges.

Pl. 36   1651. F. Cleyn. T. Warren for A. Crook.

Pl. 37   1665. W. Hollar. T. Roycroft for J. Ogilby.

Pl. 38   1666. F. Barlow. W. Godbid for F. Barlow.

Pl. 39   1531.   *Alciati.*
Anon.   H.
Steyner,
Augsburg.

Pl. 40   1534.   *Alciati.* Anon. C. Wechel,
Paris.

Pl. 41   1547. *Alciati.* B. Salomon.
J. de Tournes, Lyons.

Pl. 42   1666. F. Barlow. W. Godbid for F. Barlow.

Pl. 43   [ca. 1476]. [*1480?*]. Anon. J. Zainer, Ulm.

Pl. 44   1542. *1544*. Anon. D. Ja-   Pl. 45   1561. Anon. J. de Mar-
         not, Paris.   nef, Paris.

Pl. 46   1566. V. Solis. S. Feyerabend,
          Frankfort.

Pl. 47   1567. *1578*. M. Gheeraerts. P. de Clerck for M. Gheer-
          aerts, Bruges.

Pl. 48   1651. F. Cleyn. T. Warren for A. Crook.

Pl. 49   1665. W. Hollar. T. Roycroft for J. Ogilby.

Pl. 50   1666. F. Barlow. W. Godbid for F. Barlow.

Bibliography
Index

Bibliography

Audin, M., and Vial, E. *Dictionnaire des artistes et ouvriers d'art du Lyonnais*. Paris: Bibliothèque d'art et d'archéologie, 1918.

Benesch, Otto. *Artistic and Intellectual Trends from Rubens to Daumier As Shown in Book Illustration*. Cambridge, Mass.: Harvard University Press, 1943.

Boner, Ulrich. *Der Edelstein*. Facsimile of the undated edition in the Kgl. Bibliothek, Berlin. Introduction by Paul Kristeller. Berlin: B. Cassirer, 1908.

——. *Der Edelstein. Faksimile der ersten Druckausgabe Bamberg 1461. 16.IEth.2° der Herzog August Bibliothek Wolfenbüttel*. Introduction by Doris Fouquet. Stuttgart: Müller and Schindler, 1972.

Brun, Robert. *Le livre français illustré de la Renaissance: Étude suivie du catalogue des principaux livres à figures du XVIe siècle*. Paris: A. & J. Picard, 1969.

Cartier, Alfred. *Bibliographie des éditions des de Tournes imprimeurs Lyonnais*. Paris: Editons Bibliothèques Nationales de France, 1937.

Caxton, William. *The History and Fables of Aesop: Translated and Printed by William Caxton 1484*. Reproduced in facsimile from the unique perfect copy in the Royal Library, Windsor Castle, with an introduction by Edward Hodnett. London: The Scolar Press, 1976.

Clair, Colin. *Christopher Plantin*. London: Cassell, 1960.

Dalbanne, C., and Droz, E. *Les subtilles fables d'Esope. Notice de J. Bastin. Livres à gravures imprimés à Lyon au XVIe siècle*. Fasc. 4. Lyons: Association G. Le Roy, [1927].

Doderer, Klaus. *Fabeln: Formen Figuren Lehren*. Zurich: Atlantis, 1970.

Fischel, Lilli. *Bilderfolger in frühen Buchdruck. Studien zur Inkunabel-Illustration in Ulm und Strassburg*. Konstanz and Stuttgart: J. Thorbecke, 1963.

Geldner, Ferdinand. *Die Buchdruckerkunst im alten Bamberg 1458/59 bis 1519.* Bamberg: Meisenbach, 1964.

——. *Die deutschen Inkunabeldrucker.* Stuttgart: A. Hiersemann, 1968.

Goldschmidt, Adolph. *An Early MS of the Aesop Fables of Avianus and Related MSS.* Studies in MS Illumination, no. 1. Princeton, N.J.: Princeton University Press, 1947.

Green, Henry. *Andrea Alciati and His Book of Emblems.* London: Trübner, 1872.

Guter, Josef. "Fünfhundert Jahre Fabelillustration." *Antiquariat* 22, nos. 3, 4, 6, 7 (1972).

Hale, David G. "William Barret's *The Fables of Aesop.*" *PBSA* 64 (Third Quarter, 1970): 283–94.

——. "Aesop in Renaissance England." *The Library* 27 (June 1972): 116–25.

Henkel, A., and Schöne, A. *Emblemata: Handbuch zur Sinnbildkunst des XVI. und XVII. Jahrhunderts.* Stuttgart: J. B. Metzlersche, 1967.

Hind, A. M. *A History of Engraving & Etching.* Boston: Houghton Mifflin, 1923.

——. *An Introduction to a History of Woodcut.* Boston: Houghton Mifflin, 1935.

Hobbs, A. S. *Illustrated Fables: A Catalogue of the Library's Holdings.* Parts I & II. London: Victoria & Albert Museum, 1972. Mimeographed.

Hodnett, Edward. *Marcus Gheeraerts the Elder of Bruges, London, and Antwerp.* Utrecht: Haentjens Dekker & Gumbert, 1971.

——. *English Woodcuts 1480–1535.* Oxford: Oxford University Press, 1973. *Additions & Corrections.* Illustrated Monograph XXIIᵃ. London: The Bibliographical Society, 1973.

——. "Elisha Kirkall: First English Master of White-Line Engraving in Relief and Illustrator of Croxall's *Aesop* (1722)." *The Book Collector* 25, no. 2 (Summer 1976): 195–209.

——. *Francis Barlow: First Master of English Book Illustration.* London: The Scolar Press; Berkeley: The University of California Press, 1978.

Ivins, William M., Jr. *The Artist and the Fifteenth-Century Printer.* New York: Typophiles, 1940.

Jacobs, Joseph. *The Fables of Aesop.* London: D. Nutt, 1889.

———. *The Fables of Aesop: Selected, Told Anew, and Their History Traced.* London: Macmillan, 1894.

Keidel, George C. *A. Manual of Aesopic Fable Literature.* Baltimore: Friedenwald, 1896. To 1500.

Kristeller, Paul. *Kupferstich und Holzschnitt in vier Jahrhunderten.* Berlin: B. Cassirer, 1922.

Küster, Christian L. "Illustrierte Aesop-Ausgaben des 15. und 16. Jahrhunderts." Ph.D. diss., University of Hamburg, 1970.

Lanckorońska, Maria. "Der Zeichner der Illustrationen des Ulmer Aesop." *Gutenberg-Jahrbuch 1966,* 275–83.

Lenaghan, R. T., ed. *Caxton's* Aesop. Cambridge: Harvard University Press, 1967. Zainer's cuts substituted for Caxton's.

Lessing, Gotthold Ephraim. *Fables and Epigrams: with Essays on Fable and Epigram.* London: J. and H. L. Hunt, 1825.

McKendry, John J., ed. *Aesop: Five Centuries of Illustrated Fables.* New York: The Metropolitan Museum of Art, 1964.

Mandowsky, Erna. "Pirro Ligorio's Illustrations to Aesop's Fables." *Journal of the Warburg and Courtauld Institutes* 24 (1961): 327–31.

Monroy, Ernst F. von. *Embleme und Emblembücher in den Niederlanden 1560–1630.* Utrecht: Haentjens Dekker & Gumbert, 1964.

Morris, William. "On the Artistic Qualities of the Woodcut Books of Ulm and Augsburg in the Fifteenth Century." *Bibliographica* 1 (1895): 437–73.

Mortimer, Ruth, ed. *French 16th Century Books.* Cambridge: Harvard University Press, 1964.

———. *Italian 16th Century Books.* Cambridge: Harvard University Press, 1974.

Croft-Murray, Edward, and Hulton, Paul. *Catalogue of British Drawings in the British Museum.* London: The Trustees of the British Museum, 1960.

Newbigging, Thomas. *Fables and Fabulists: Ancient & Modern.* London: E. Stock, 1895.

Novotný, Miloslav, ed. *Ezop Václava Hollara.* Prague: Sfinx, 1936. Reproduces all of Hollar's plates for Ogilby's *Aesop Paraphras'd* (1665).

Ogilby, John. *The Fables of Aesop* (1668). Introduction by E. Miner. Los Angeles: William Andrews Clark Memorial Library, 1965. Reproduces the 1665 plates reduced.

Perry, Ben E. *Babrius and Phaedrus*. London and Cambridge, Mass.: Loeb Classical Library, 1965.

Plessow, Max. *Geschichte des Fabeldichtung in England bis zu John Gay (1726)*. Berlin: Mayer & Müller, 1906.

Pollard, A. W. *Early Illustrated Books*. London: Kegan Paul, Trench, Trübner, 1917.

Praz, Mario. *Studies in Seventeenth-Century Imagery*. Rome: Edizioni di storia e letteratura, 1964.

Quinnan, Barbara. *Fables: From Incunabula to Modern Picture Books. A Selective Bibliography*. Washington, D.C.: Library of Congress, 1966.

Rooses, Max. *Christophe Plantin*. Antwerp: J. Maes, 1890.

Ruelens, C., and De Backer, A. *Annales de l'imprimerie Plantinienne*. Brussels: F. Heussner, 1865.

Scheler, Lucien. "La persistance du motif dans l'illustration des fables d'Esope du seizième et dix-septième siècle." In *Studia Bibliographica in honorem Herman de La Fontaine Verwey*. Amsterdam: Menno Hertzberger, 1966.

Schlumberger, Camille. *Promenade au jardin des fables*. Paris: Braun and Berger-Levrault, 1923.

Schuchard, Margret. *John Ogilby (1600–1676): Lebensbild eines Gentleman mit vielen Karrieren*. Hamburg: P. Hartung, 1973.

——. *A Descriptive Bibliography of the Works of John Ogilby and William Morgan*. Bern: H. Lang; Frankfurt, P. Lang, 1975.

Schulz, Herbert C. "Albrecht Pfister and the Nürnberg Woodcut School." *Gutenberg-Jahrbuch 1953*, 36–49.

Strahm, Hans. "Ulrich Boner's *Edelstein:* A Mediaeval Book of Fables from the Time of the Minnesinger." *Graphis* 1 (April, June 1945): 197–98.

Thiele, Georg, ed. *Der illustrierte lateinische Aesop in der Handschrift des Ademar. Codex Vossianus. Lat. Oct. 15. Fol. 195–205*. Leiden: A. W. Sijthoff, 1905.

Tiemann, Barbara. *Fabel und Form: Gilles Corrozet und die französische Renaissance Fabel*. Munich: W. Fink, 1974.

Tiemann, H. "Wort and Bild in der Fabeltradition bis zu La

Fontaine." In *Buch and Welt: Festschrift für Gustav Hofmann*. Wiesbaden: O. Harrossowitz, 1965.

Van Eerde, Katherine S. *Wenceslaus Hollar: Delineator of His Time*. Charlottesville: University Press of Virginia for The Folger Shakespeare Library, 1970.

———. *John Ogilby and the Taste of His Times*. Folkstone: Dawson, 1976.

Weil, Ernst. *Der Ulmer Holzschnitt im 15. Jahrhundert*. Berlin: Mauritius-Verlag, 1923.

Worringer, Wilhelm. *Die altdeutsche Buchillustration*. Munich: R. Piper, 1921.

Index